HILDA

June 25th 2012

For Adrian
Mirabellii

Hilda Pierce

HILDA

✦

A True Story of Terror, Tears and Triumph

Hilda Pierce

iUniverse, Inc.

New York Lincoln Shanghai

HILDA
A True Story of Terror, Tears and Triumph

iUniverse books may be ordered through booksellers or by contacting:

iUniverse
2021 Pine Lake Road, Suite 100
Lincoln, NE 68512
www.iuniverse.com
1-800-Authors (1-800-288-4677)

The views expressed in this work are solely those of the author and do not necessarily reflect the views of the publisher, and the publisher hereby disclaims any responsibility for them.

ISBN: 978-0-595-42530-3 (pbk)

ISBN: 978-0-595-86859-9 (ebk)

Printed in the United States of America

For my husband Herman
and
my granddaughter Melissa

"In order to be a realist,
you have to believe in miracles"

David Ben Gurion

Contents

In gratitude

I am indebted to the following people, who with their enthusiasm, kindness and generosity in giving of their valuable time, helped to make my book more readable:

Don Harrison, my editor prevented me from giving up when I was discouraged, was always patient and kind and worked hard to help me organize my story.

Sherilin Heise, was an incredible helpmate and worked for hours trying to find my many lost paragraphs on my computer. Miraculously she always knew where to conjure them up again. Without her I could never have gotten to the end of my book.

Sonia Lesser and Blair Richwood, whose positive input and help gave me a boost and a desire to make my book a reality.

Jan Pierce, unsolicited and so highly professional made some very needed suggestions and corrections.

Kenneth Martin Pierce, whose thorough and frank critique made me sit up and listen. I referred to it many times and learned from it.

Brian Schottlaender, deserves a special thank you for his friendship and assistance in trying to find a publisher for me.

Frances and Ken Venn, friends extra-ordinaire came to the rescue at the very end with a last read-through.

Todd Michaud, my computer guru who helped me so very much to submit my book to my publisher for me. He came to the rescue in all my emergencies.

Ron Amack, my iUniverse contact PSA, always helpful, patient and available.

Herman Slutzky, my husband deserves a special *medal of honor* for never threatening to leave home, when I drove him crazy with my cries for help:" Herman, my computer stopped again. I am afraid I lost everything and I have worked so hard. I do so love and appreciate you."

Comments about the Book

Don Harrison
Author, Publisher, Editor
San Diego, California
"Although Hilda is a painter by profession, she easily could have pursued a successful literary career. Hilda has the artist's eye for detail and color. As a reader, you can picture the events in her remarkable life as she narrates them–so visual are some of her descriptions. By the time I concluded editing it, I didn't just feel I knew Hilda, I felt as if I also knew the many people who were part of her life, and felt that I had traveled along side on her life's journey."

Frederick Seitz
President Emeritus, Rockefeller University,
Past President, National Academy of Sciences
New York, N.Y.
"I am awaiting the revised version of your manuscript. Actually, I have read through the first version which I found fascinating much as it stands and would not feel that much heavy editing is really needed.
Incidentally, I discussed the nature of your book with an old friend, at the University of San Francisco (a Nobel prize laureate). He expressed much interest in the work particularly after I gave him an outline of the situation it describes. All best wishes Sincerely,"
Fred

The Rev.Canon **Jack E. Lindquist**
St. Paul's Cathedral, San Diego
"I can honestly tell you (and not just to be nice) that I was absolutely fascinated with your story. It is the kind of personal story-telling that not only relates an individual's life with real literary skill, but also sets that experience within a tremendous world-historical drama that was unfolding at the same time. I find this fusion of the intimate and the international to be completely absorbing because the one illuminates the other".

General **Hank Darmstandler**
San Diego
"This story has all of the compelling, conflicting and converging elements of human endeavor that separate the worldly from the commonplace, the magnificent from the mundane. It is a story of a resourceful young girl growing into a continuingly resourceful, courageous and extremely talented great lady. A lady who has earned happiness the hard way, she has just made it happen."

Deborah Szekely
Founder, Owner of Rancho la Puerta
Tecate, Mexico
"I so much enjoyed reading your manuscript. I picked it up intending to spend a half hour reading, and was so intrigued that I spent my whole Sunday reading it cover to cover. It is nice to know a survivor, and even nicer to know a survivor with lots of luck. Your timing has been so fortuitous, you are a miracle."

Erica Torri
Director Atheneum Music and Arts Library
La Jolla, California
"I read your story with great interest and enthusiasm. You have had an extraordinary and wonderful life. Full of tragic and scary events, but then saved by your savvy and the many special people around you who recognized the flame in you.
What a special account of all these years. I can't believe in what detail you are able to recall people and events and places. I read it all in one sitting and could not stop. I enjoyed the story of your life and thanks again for bringing it to my attention."

Constance Broomfield
Broomfield International
Washington D.C.
"This is the story of an extraordinary woman. She is a with-it ahead of her time, inspirational woman in her 80's. She escaped on her own at age sixteen from Nazi Europe and made her way to Chicago, by way of England. These chapters of her life, as are the subsequent ones are so remarkable, she speaks of them with such staggering clarity, warmth and humor. She has lectured all over the world and still gives amazing lectures today. Hilda has also created a remarkable body of art work and is said to have had one of the largest art commissions for any artist. 1,400 paintings for two Mega Cruise ships of Carnival Cruise Lines. Hilda keeps me spellbound."

Judge **Toby Gerst**
Phoenix, Arizona

"I'm immersed in your book. I think it is wonderful, it is so hard to put it down. It is a fine work. It is different from the template of a novel, yet it reads as though the reader lives alongside you in parallel time. Would you mind if I propose it to read in my book group? This is so engaging."

Jill Marsal
Del Mar, California
"**Sandra Dijkstra** and I read your manuscript and she asked me to contact you as I have worked with a number of manuscripts about the holocaust and that time period. We discussed your work and were really taken with it. You write very well and have amazing detail. Your account of the pre-war years in Vienna is very interesting, as are your experiences and I personally enjoyed reading this as did Sandy."

Preface

What follows is "Hilda," a true story of terror, tears and triumph. All the characters are real people, though some names were changed to protect their privacy. The story begins in 1938 Vienna, Austria. It is important to mention that Austria was the second largest European country before World War I.

Known as the Austro-Hungarian Monarchy it included all of Hungary, parts of Poland, Italy, Czechoslovakia and Yugoslavia, with a population of sixty-four million people. After Austria lost World War I in 1918, the Versailles Treaty reduced the country to the city of Vienna and the mountains of the Alps going west. Almost no flat land was left on which to grow grain for food.

Austria's population was now only six million starving people. The Monarchy ended and Austria became a Democratic Republic. The war had been costly and decimated a large number of the male population. Vienna, the city of my birth, was a sad gray city, where war veterans were begging on street corners in tattered uniforms. The years of the twenties and thirties were turbulent times in Austria. Political parties were fighting each other, a civil war, a depression, unemployment, food shortages and the assassination of Dollfuss, the Chancellor of Austria, were some of the events during my childhood.

In March 1938, Adolf Hitler and his hordes paraded into Austria and swept the tiny nation into the third Reich.

I was sixteen years old at the time, and that is where my story begins.

Eveline and Hilda

My mother and I both were present as girls for the triumphal tours of world leaders in Austria. The occasions, some forty years apart, could not have been more different.

Mutti, as mothers are affectionately called in German, then was known by her given name of Eveline. She had been chosen to present Emperor Franz Josef of the Austro-Hungarian Empire with a bouquet of flowers, to recite a poem, and then finish her performance with a deep curtsy on the day that his train pulled into the village of Lassee. It was a short distance from Vienna and the Czech and Hungarian borders.

At the time of Kaiser Franz Josef's visit, Eveline was somewhere between eight and ten years old, so the date might have been anywhere between 1898 or 1900. The Empress Elizabeth had been assassinated in 1897. That coupled with the murder suicide of his mistress by his only son, Rudolph, the Crown Prince in Mayerling, the decade before had left Franz Josef a very depressed man. In 1900 the emperor would have been seventy years old.

Lassee was about thirty miles east of Vienna, enroute to Marchegg, a larger town, sort of a county seat, as well as to Bratislava, Czechoslovakia, at that time still part of the Austro-Hungarian Empire. However, when it comes to the details of Eveline's part in this little drama, we know much because Mutti could still recall that scene vividly in her later years. She described her ruffled white dress, the large straw hat with a black velvet ribbon on it and her long white gloves. She had picked the flowers for the Kaiser from her father's fields: red poppies, blue cornflowers, white daisies and sheaves of wheat.

The hundred and twenty townspeople were all waiting at the railroad station that Lassee shared with another little town called Schoenfeld. With much tooting and hooting, smoke billowing from the great chimney of the engine, the train pulled in. The royal coach-door opened, the Kaiser and his retinue stood in the doorway. But they did not descend the stairs.

How was Eveline to present the bouquet? The mayor of Lassee took her by the hand, made her go up two steps of the royal coach and recite her poem. She could not curtsy because it might have caused her to fall down. The Kaiser smiled at her through his funny mustache and then she handed him the flowers but he never said a word. Mutti was very proud of that day in her young life.

In just a generation, matters can change so dramatically.

German troops marched into Austria on March twelve, 1938, effecting the union of the two-German speaking countries. The "Anschluss" was accomplished and Adolf Hitler flew to Munich and then proceeded from city to city in Austria until he reached Vienna. That is where I lived with my parents, Eveline and Julius Harmel.

Mobs of hoodlums and youths and other Nazi sympathizers filled Vienna's streets, chanting, screeching and yelling Nazi slogans: *"Heil Hitler! Sieg Heil! Down with the Jews!"* We could hear them from our apartment throughout the night, as well as on every radio report.

When Hitler was about to enter Vienna, I decided I had to go and see him at all costs. While my parents were glued to the radio, I went to my room to get my coat, hat and gloves and snuck out of the house. It was about two or three o'clock in the afternoon. I ran to the Opera in about fifteen minutes; there were huge crowds already standing along the Ringstrasse. Wending my way through the mob, I got to the curb pressed against others like a sardine in a can. People held Nazi flags and were singing the *Horst Wessel* song with its chilling lyrics about Jewish blood spurting from their knives.

Everyone was pushing, shouting, singing, and yelling. It was deafening. It was also cold and windy and I was worried I might be trampled by the mob. Even if I had wanted to return home, I could not have left. It seemed that hours and hours went by as tanks and trucks and soldiers marched past us until finally the yelling and screaming and screeching reached a level that I thought would cause my eardrums to burst. Hitler's Mercedes staff car was slowly coming toward us.

There he was standing up with his arm raised in his salute and all the people around me raising their arms and shrieking *"Heil Hitler!* *"Heil Fuehrer!"* *"Wir danken unsern Fuehrer,"* *"Die Saujuden nach*

Dachau," "*Wilkommen Hitler,*" "*Ein Reich, Ein Volk, Ein Fuehrer.*" Some were laughing, some were crying, some fell to their knees, some threw kisses, some were jumping up and down, and some were throwing flowers. It was a grotesque ballet.

I was frozen in fear and horror and felt faint and weak. Somehow I worked my way out of the thinning mob, and stumbled home all the way to the Weyringerhof, our apartment building. My parents were very upset. I could see that my mother's eyes were red and swollen, and my father was speechless for the first time since I knew him. In my desire to witness history, I had caused them great anxiety.

You see, we were Jews. What I, as an impulsive sixteen-year-old had done, had been thoughtless indeed. Had I been recognized as a Jew, I might have been killed in all that frenzy. However, spontaneity was part of my nature, and it has remained so right until today.

But over the years there had been many little Jewish girls like Eveline who had been treated with affection by their Gentile neighbors, and many Jewish adults like her father, my grandfather, Adolf Kohn, who had been well liked and respected by his townspeople, notwithstanding the fact that they were Jews. Perhaps that affection and respect accorded to some of us contributed to our undoing. Many of us—particularly those in my parents' generation—could not believe that Hitler was anything more than a passing phase.

In front of their Home
Adolf & Therese Kohn
Hilda's maternal Grandparents

Eveline and Julius Harmel
Hilda's Parents

A farm family in Lassee

Both my maternal grandparents were born in Bruenn, also known as Brno, in German-speaking Moravia, today part of the Czech Republic. Adolph Kohn was born a twin in 1858 into a family in which he had siblings who were triplets. Therese Schlesinger was born two years later, in 1860, one of *ten* children whose father was wealthy enough to engage a live-in teacher to educate all of them. Therese had a sizeable dowry and I imagine that it was with that money she and Grandpa Adolf acquired their first farm parcel in Lassee. They moved there almost immediately after their wedding in approximately 1885. I never met any of the families that they left behind in Moravia.

Grandpa invested their money wisely, using profits from the farm to acquire more and more land throughout the town of Lassee. He built a lovely house on Lassee's only paved street. The town's doctor lived next door and the church was a short block away. Although Grandpa could be stern, especially in the eyes of a precocious grand-daughter, he was very gentle and loving to Grandmother Therese, whom he called "Resi."

Yes, his wealth grew, but Grandpa never put on airs. He was very humble and spent time in the pubs with the other farmers, arm wrestling or playing cards with them. He played Tarot and chess and let them win. At harvest time, the population of Lassee would more than double with Czech-speaking farm workers who would return home after the crops were brought in. Grandfather raised more than 100 dairy cows, and a stable full of horses. He farmed all the beautiful fields from which Mutti, born in 1890, later would gather the wildflowers for the Emperor's bouquet.

Mutti had a he-goat named Kreuzer, after the Austrian coin of the time, and eleven she-goats, which would queue under her window every afternoon and wait for her to milk them. Her favorite was Bambi, the smallest one. Eveline's classmates teased her about the goat scent that clung to her clothes. She was a tomboy, much to Grandmother Therese's distress. When she was seven years old, she disappeared for long enough to cause 'Grosspapa' to go searching for her. After finding the attic door and the trap door to the roof open, he found her happily straddling the roof to inspect the stork's nest. He lured her down by promising to take her to the Prater in Vienna the following Sunday, the famous amusement park with the giant Ferris wheel.

But Mutti was attracted to far more than Vienna's Ferris wheel. Utterly charmed by the city, she persuaded her parents to let her attend school there. She fell in love with the city's music, culture and beautiful shops, and although she returned to the farm in Lassee after twelve years in Vienna, she knew that she was destined some-day to return there.

In the meantime, however, Emperor Franz Josef suffered another violent death in his family when, in 1914, his nephew and heir to the crown, the Archduke Ferdinand, was assassinated in Sarajevo,

Bosnia-Herzogovina. Mutti's sister, Camilla, lived in that city with her husband Jacob Gruenwald, who was a mining engineer. It was a matter of remarkable coincidence that my aunt Camilla and my four-year-old cousin Erich were standing close enough to the Archduke's passing car on June twenty-eight, 1914, to personally witness the assassination that historians mark as the catalyst for the First World War. Beyond the fact that they were there, however, nothing of what they saw that fateful day has been passed down to us.

The emperor blamed the assassination on the separatist group, the Black Hand, which wanted to leave the Austro-Hungarian Empire and merge with Serbia. He demanded that Serbia turn over the members of the Black Hand who were responsible. Germany said it would support the Austrian emperor if he decided to take reprisals. The Serbians appealed to the Russians for protection.

The dominos of war kept falling. Even in Lassee, Mutti's younger brother, Karl, had to go into military service at age sixteen. Mutti became grandfather's right hand in the running of the farm. Austria's military forces had some early successes, and the government sent eighty Russian prisoners of war to be laborers on our family's farm. Mutti knew Czech and some Russian, enough to communicate with the workers.

The fortunes of war turned, however. All Austrians were asked to give up their gold jewelry and to trade it in for an iron medal with the inscription, "*I gave gold for iron.*" The greatest sacrifice for our family was that young Karl came home with a bullet in his lung, a wound received in 1915 during the great battle at the Isonzo River in Italy. He lived long enough to marry and father a son named Walter, but died as a consequence of that bullet at age twenty-eight.

Throughout Austria, but particularly in Vienna, food became extremely scarce during the war and a number of years thereafter. Many people sought to barter produce for jewelry or other of their possessions directly from the farms, including that of my grandparents. One such woman who came from Vienna every week befriended the family. With her eye on Eveline, the pretty daughter of the wealthy farmer, she told my grandparents about her nephew Julius Harmel, a university-educated, charming young man of twenty-nine. After fighting in Russia, he had returned to Vienna at the end of the war. My grandparents politely invited the woman and her nephew to come back the following week for *"Jause"* the afternoon refreshment time.

Mutti had spurned all the young suitors who were farmers in Lassee because she did not want to spend the rest of her life on a farm. She was determined to someday live in Vienna. When my mother was teenager, it had been the custom for parents to start preparing a hope chest full of clothes and household linens for their daughter's future wedding—still single at age twenty-eight the family thought she might never marry. But she merely was exercising her prerogative to choose a husband carefully.

Eveline was immediately drawn to the soft-spoken, genteel city boy who invited her to come see a Viennese Opera with him the following Saturday. She served coffee and cake with whipped cream, making certain to serve Julius an extra large portion. No longer used to rich food—as all food was scarce in Vienna—poor Julius felt sick from the treat, but didn't want to let on. Surreptitiously he put the whipped cream into his hanky, and his hanky into his pocket. Later, as they walked around the large courtyard to the stables, Mutti saw the melted cream running down his pants. As he explained why his pockets were *"mit Schlag"* they both burst out laughing. It was the start of their romance.

For Austria, generally, however, the war had brought little to smile about. By 1918, Austria clearly was the loser. With the signing of the Treaty of Versailles in June 1919, the Austro-Hungarian Empire was shorn of Hungary, Czechoslovakia, a northern section of Italy, and parts of Poland—the number of its inhabitants declined from 64 million to 6 million starving people. Wounded war veterans with missing limbs begged in their tattered uniforms on Vienna street corners. Homeless people dug holes in the ground at the outskirts of the city and lived in them. While Austria still could claim the large city of Vienna and a large region of the Alps (where little food could be grown), it was left with only one good agricultural region. It was called the "Corn Chamber of Austria," east of Vienna, where my grandparents had their farm.

Grandpa Adolf was not very happy as Mutti's romance with Julius blossomed. He tried to talk her out of a marriage until the very last minute. But on September 19, 1919, he lost his fine farm manager daughter whose heart was set on living in the big city. Following their wedding, Mutti and Julius moved to Vienna. There they began married life in the same building as my paternal grandparents, my father's sister, Adele, Max and their son Fritz and some other cousins.

Julius's parents—my paternal grandparents—had been born in Poland's German-speaking area in Lemberg, a city called Lvov by the Poles. Both were orphans, though they had aunts and uncles, who did not want the responsibility of looking after them. They urged these children to get married at an early age. My grandfather, Moses Aaron Harmel, was only fifteen and my grandmother, Rosa Sperber, only fourteen at their wedding. Each carried a little cardboard suitcase, and a small amount of money their relatives had collected for them when they left for Vienna.

My grandfather, who was known as "Mo" throughout his life, was a very smart young man with a good Jewish education but no secular schooling. With the little money they had, he bought small antiques or old pretty things, then sold them when and where he could. In 1877, he was successful enough to found an antique store. He learned quickly and called himself an "autodidact." (A learned word to describe a self-taught man). Grandpa Mo fathered eleven children, my father being the youngest, born in 1888

Hilda and her Mother 1924

Hilda age 16

Hilda in America 1940

Hilda Age 25

A Vienna Childhood

My father, had a lifetime contract position with the Austrian Railroad system, but Mutti thought there would be a better future for them if he would work in Grandfather Harmel's antique store. The railroad offered a steady salary, true, but the terrible inflation caused money to be devalued daily. The prices, and profits, from antiques could be adjusted to the economy, whereas father's railroad salary was fixed. Mutti understood that before long such a salary would become almost worthless. Eventually father acquiesced to her wishes.

I was born July eight, 1921. After a brief period for recuperation, Mutti resumed helping Papa in the store. My parents took over ownership of the antique store even before Grandma Rosa died in 1922 and Grandpa Mo in 1923.

The store truly was filled with treasures. At one time they had a bedroom set of the Austrian princess, Marie Antoinette. It came into their hands at the end of the Austrian Monarchy, when all the furnishings and art from the Kaiser's palaces went up for auction.

I frequently was left in the care of Mitzi, my mother's favorite maid who had moved with her from Lassee to Vienna. Mitzi took good care of me, often carrying me about in papoose-like pillow contraption called a *Steckkissen*. I also was transported in a large baby car-

riage with wheels almost as big as a small bicycle's. I
lace curtains on the collapsible hood.

Mitzi loved to walk me to the Schweizergarten near the Belvedere
Palace, which had been one of the homes of the Austrian Chancellor. The Schweizergarten had a beautiful rose garden and a large
open area for children to play. We went there every afternoon.

Sometimes we walked to the other end of the Schweizergarten
where there was an outdoor restaurant. My parents would meet us
after the 6 p.m. closing of the antique store. I loved the soft drinks
that came in a glass bottle. It had a glass marble that needed to be
pushed down into the bottle's neck in order to access the fizzy sweet
drink.

In the winter, the open area was covered with water that froze over
for a skating rink. I often went skating there although my ankles
were weak and I could never learn to execute a proper figure-8.
Mutti knitted heavy woolen stockings for me and Mitzi helped me
put on my skates after putting bandages on my ankles. Mutti and
Mitzi were co-anchors of my young life.

Vendors sold hot drinks, including tea with rum in it, and even sold
it to children. It was sweet and hot and made me feel warm and
wonderful. A loudspeaker played music and we waltzed on the ice.
When I was older, I was allowed to go to the artificial ice rink.
Many times, we watched Sonja Henie, the star skater, practicing her
programs there. She often came to Vienna. The lanterns in the park

were gaslights, when the lamplighter arrived, at dusk, it was our sig-
nal to go home for supper.

The gardens of the Belvedere palace stood apart from the Schweizergarten. They were designed in the French style, with tightly clipped
hedges, ponds and fountains. There were large sculptures of
sphinxes with heads and breasts of women while the rest of the bod-
ies were those of lions. I recall climbing on them and riding the
sphinxes as my magical horses. In front of the palace was a huge
pond filled with carp, which were such lazy fish they also put an
electric eel into the water to chase the carps around. Were it not for
the eel, they would have gotten fatter and fatter lying at the bottom
of the pond. Carp is the traditional Christmas dinner fish. Mutti
would send Mitzi to the outdoor Market to buy the fish live from
open barrels. I always accompanied her and dreaded the time when
the fish were hacked into pieces. Sometimes when the fish were
being boiled the tail portion would still wiggle and lift the pot-lid,
which I thought revolting. Never to this day, have I been able to eat
carp.

The palace itself was once the residence of Prinz Eugen, but long
since has housed an art gallery that features Gustav Klimt's paintings.

Our home was in the Weyringer Hof, a once beautiful and famous
complex of four five-story buildings where the sculptor Franz
Zelesny and Maler Kempf, a well-known painter of religious subjects, also lived. As a result of such artists having their *ateliers, or* studios, in the building, Kaiser Franz Josef himself had once visited the

premises. To commemorate that event, a bronze bust of the emperor was placed in our garden on a mound of earth covered with ivy.

Christmas Eve 1928: Dusk hung over the courtyard garden, and the surrounding apartment buildings loomed large and ominous against the gray winter sky. The old cotton-wood tree whose limbs reached to the fifth story, was bare. It's branches were covered with snow. Lanterns leading to the back apartments and up the steps were not yet lit.

In a small group, we children—all of us bundled in heavy scarves and coats and thick, clumsy woolen underwear–were jumping off the steps to keep warm and to compete. Who could jump off the eighth step without falling? Twice I had sprained my ankles. "Mutti" (mother) had to bathe them and put on bandages. She put some granules into the water that made it purple, smelled sour and supposedly had some healing powers. But I kept on with the jumping competition.

There was Toni, a tall blond girl a few years older than I; her little brother, Ernst; the two daughters of the building superintendent, Mitzi and Trude; Herbert, a young giant (he was the oldest of the bunch); my closest friend, Nora, who spoke Hungarian with her mother; and my cousin Fritz, who lived in the apartment above ours. Next to little Ernst, I was the youngest–about six then.

In all, 20 children lived in our complex, named Weyringerhof, and we played together almost daily. Sometimes we were knights in shining armor. Then we were in U-boats, with Herbert, of course, as the captain. In the fall we built fortresses out of the fallen leaves and defended our honor with wooden swords. Oh, what an enchanted world we had in that garden!

Often, when we played hide-and-seek, I'd crouch behind the emperor's statue, shivering and shaking, because at any moment I knew I would be confronted with the ghost of Franz Josef. I could almost hear the rustle of his robe and see he handlebars of his moustache.

Austria then was a very small and poor republic. But none of us children felt poor; we had a very rich and imaginative life in that garden.

Earlier that afternoon I had been invited by my friend Trude's parents to help decorate their Christmas tree. All decorations were edible, homemade cookies, icicles filled with sugar water, tiny chocolate bottles filled with sweet liqueurs, walnuts and other nuts in little mesh bags, and strings of figs and other dried fruits. Many decorations never reached the tree. We had a wonderful time.

Later that day we waited outside with our cold, red noses for the Christmas trees to be lit. All the trees stood by the windows and had little wax candles clipped onto the branches. One by one the windows were aglow with circlets of candlelight, flickering in the dusk, casting pink and yellow reflections on the snow-covered windowsills.

Suddenly a glow brighter than the light of the candles blazed from the second floor window of Major Baumgartner's home. The curtains were on fire! The windows were thrown open, and a huge billow of smoke escaped toward the sky. The fire department came with a great clanging of bells, and the fire was put out. The firemen had a busy night; fires like this occurred all over the city.

One by one my friends went home to their own celebrations.

In my Jewish home there was no tree. I sat by my window with my nose pressed hard against the icy pane, my breath making clear spots on the frozen glass. All over the building the candles glowed, shining brighter and brighter as the night became darker.

Later that night, our maid, Mitzi, awakened me. She bundled me up and we walked together through the icy streets to St. Stephen's Cathedral in the center of Vienna. The Cardinal of Austria himself conducted Midnight Mass. His garments and his priest's robes were all covered with gold embroidery. Thousands of beeswax candles created a light smoke and the scent of those candles and the incense filled the air in the enormous cavern of the cathedral. On the altar the Monstranz glistened with hundreds of diamonds, rubies, emeralds and gold. Pine garlands and flowers were everywhere. Suddenly, the organ and the choir burst out in song. It was an awsome, thrilling spectacle-one I knew I would always remember.

When Mass was over Mitzi and I rode the crowded streetcar home.

1938:
My old friends from the Weyringerhof were marching past me in Nazi uniforms to the sound of the Horst Wessel song. "When Jewish blood will spurt from our knives."

They had forgotten that I was their friend.

Our apartment had two bedrooms, a large living room that also served as a dining room, a kitchen, foyer and a bathroom. Our walls were painted by special artist painters who used all kinds of methods to bring out the beauty of their patterns. They used stencils, sprays, and some metallic paints. The walls were very beautiful.

There were no closets. In Vienna, we used wooden wardrobes. In that my father was in the antique furniture business, our wardrobes had very beautiful wood with gorgeous markings that had to be highly polished. There was one wardrobe in each bedroom and another very large one that took up a whole wall in the foyer.

Our living room walls featured a design of chestnut leaves and chestnuts in tones of beige and gold. They immediately brought to mind the wide avenue called Haupt-Allee that was lined with chestnut trees. Songs were written about the blooming of these trees on that avenue leading to a royal chalet in the Prater.

Above the table, in the middle of the living room, was a chandelier that had a huge silk lampshade with fringe. It could be pulled up or down for the times when we ate or when I did homework at that table. There was a wall of bookcases with glass doors and hundreds of books. A sofa and several round armchairs stood on a Persian carpet that covered almost the entire parquet wood floor. My Boesendorfer piano stood near the windows. There were four large framed photographs of my grandparents, and some wonderful museum copies in oil paint of Brueghels and Spitzweg on the walls.

My room had a Thonet rocking chair, and a brass bed with pink curtains on each end of it. The mattresses were filled with horsehair and were hard, but we had pillows and huge down covers that felt like oversized pillows. My wardrobe was painted white. My light fixture had three hanging glass globes with pink and clear glass patterns, each on a different length of pink silk rope. A white dressing table with an oval mirror and a white chair with a pink petit point cushion completed the room's furnishings.

My parents' bedroom had blond wood furniture. Over the bed was a painting by Waldmueller of a woman suckling an infant.

The kitchen had a gas stove, a kitchen table and chairs, and, behind a curtain, a folding bed and dresser for Mitzi. We did not have a refrigerator or an icebox. There was a lovely washstand with a beautiful china basin and a matching pitcher below on the shelf.

Our dishes were Rosenthal china and the silverware was larger than that of other countries. Our tablecloths were white linen damask with openwork *ajour* that had been made by hand by the workers on my grandparents' farm. The napkins were very large and we used napkin rings. We had a cruet stand of crystal with a toothpick holder, tiny crystal salt cellars with tiny spoons, and a footed crystal bowl with fruit in the center of the table.

Our entry door had glass with wrought iron covering the glass. Our windows came in double sets. One opened into the room, the other out of the room. In the winter, we had stuffed pillows between the windows to keep out the cold drafts. For heating, we had a huge tiled, coal burning stove that looked like a small castle.

From age three to first grade, I was enrolled in a private nursery school where we called the teacher "Aunt." Tante Schneider took our entire class to the Belvedere to have us photographed on the steps of the palace.

I vividly recall a humiliating event in that nursery school class that occurred at the beginning of my tenure there as a three-year-old. I had an "accident"—that is, I wet my pants—and Tante Schneider called the maid, who came with sawdust and dustpan and swept the floor under my seat. She removed my pants and hung them for all to see on the tile-covered stove that stood in front of the class. I never got over this embarrassment and, as a result, I never liked the three years that I spent in nursery school.

We did learn a lot, nevertheless, as the kindergarten was patterned after a Montessori school, which then was the trendy new rage. We learned to use a potato peeler, to knit, and to crochet. By age five, I had learned to knit socks and maneuver five knitting needles to turn a heel.

The Nursery School was only two doors away from our building and I was allowed to walk home by myself. While crossing the garden to walk to our apartment, I sometimes saw the sculptor Franz Zelesny working on a large marble sculpture of a chariot drawn by winged horses ascending toward heaven in bas-relief. It was fascinating for me to see how his chisel could coax a figure out of the marble. When I asked him how he knew what was inside the marble, he'd smile and say: "Oh they are all locked up inside, just waiting for me to let them come out." Sometimes he would stop chiseling and invite me into his Studio and give me some wet clay and show me how to make little angels. By the time I was five I could actually make some that could almost be recognized as little dolls with wings.

The painter, Herr Kempf, who was famous for his beautiful madonnas and other religious art, lived in another part of our building. He also allowed me to visit him and let me watch him paint in his large living room that he used as his workroom. He even let me hold his palette with mounds of all the colors on it. He showed me how to put my thumb into the provided hole to firmly grip the tablet. Holding his palette made me feel very proud. At times he would lift me onto his stool and put a brush into my right hand. Oh, how I wanted to dip it into the oil colors and start painting! He, however, would take the palette and brush from me, mix two colors together and they became a new color; then I would be allowed to do that also. How wonderful it was to mix the cobalt blue with the bright yellow; before our eyes the color would turn to a bright green. When the artist took the palette and brush from me to use the color I had made for his canvas, I was thrilled. He smiled and went on painting. I knew it was time for me to go home.

I'd run two steps at a time, down the four flights of stairs, and then take a shortcut through the garden so I could run into our store to tell Papa about my adventures. It was clear to me, even though I was not even in first grade, that my destiny was to be an artist.

The owner of our apartment house had a handsome young grandson in his early twenties. Tall blond and blue-eyed, driving a huge American car, a maroon Plymouth (1936?), he'd come to visit his grandfather often. I must have been five or six when I first began to take notice of Paul passing by me as I was jumping rope, playing ball or playing games with the other children who lived in our complex. Later on I became acutely aware of Paul, who most of time carried a briefcase under his left arm so that his right hand would be ready to pinch my cheek as he said: "Hurry little Hilda, grow up fast so I can marry you." I would feel my cheeks start to get hot and red, knowing that my friends would laugh and tease me for hours afterwards with:" Hilda has a boyfriend, Hilda has a boyfriend." How prescient they were! In truth Paul was my idol, my movie star, and not withstanding our great difference in age, I was determined to marry him, if it were to take a hundred years.

We lived next door to Paul's grandfather. He claimed the owner's privilege of occupying the only flat with a balcony in the entire building complex. It was supported by two caryatids, pillars in the shape of women. They fascinated me every time I walked between them to the door leading to our home.

My father's sister Adele took me to enroll in the first grade, as Mutti and Papa were busy at the store. She made an appointment with the school principal. She told him that I already knew how to read. Adele asked if I could skip one class and go directly into second grade, but the principal said he did not approve of "skipping" so I started school with the other six-year-olds. At the time, I resented the Vienna principal's decision, but, later when I had a daughter of my own, I came to understand his wisdom. She skipped not once, but twice, and while she was academically excellent, I felt that she was socially handicapped by being so young.

In Vienna, all incoming school children received their first reading book as a gift from the city government. After that, we had to buy our schoolbooks. For writing, we used little framed slates with chalk. Because Austria was a Catholic country, there were crucifixes in every classroom. A priest came into our class at ten a.m. every morning to teach catechism. I was the only Jewish child in the class. Rather than making me leave the room, he had me sit in the back row during the session. Of course, I learned right along with the Catholic children, but when I would raise my hand to answer a question—which I often did—the priest always said, "not you, Harmel."

On Wednesday afternoons, a Lutheran girl and I were both excused from our class to go to a different school where we could receive instruction in our respective religions. Children from other schools also gathered there. We had a rabbi who taught us biblical history and ancient Hebrew prayers; unfortunately they were never translated into German for us. We did not understand their meaning. On Saturday mornings we were obligated to attend Sabbath services at our synagogue. In Austria, all synagogues were Orthodox. Women sat in the balcony and the men prayed together downstairs. We didn't understand a word of that either.

The only time I can remember enjoying being at the synagogue was during Chanukah, when we children received a little bag containing candy, an orange and some walnuts. Oranges in winter were a luxury. My mother went to synagogue only on the High Holidays of Rosh Hashanah and Yom Kippur, when my Grandmother Kohn would come to visit from Lassee. Mutti would dutifully accompany her to the services in the *Musikverein Saal*, the large famous concert hall downtown.

In those days, between the wars, we would often go to the Vienna Woods on summer Sundays where we would hike and have picnics. Mutti scrupulously packed extra food to share with the poor people one would always encounter there. We were very fortunate. We always had food because on many weekends we would take a train to my grandparent's home in Lassee and return to Vienna with suitcases filled with meats, cheese and vegetables. Sometimes we lugged sacks of flour, sugar and potatoes. I often brought different children home to share our big midday meal because they rarely saw meat in their own homes and we often shared our food with our friends and neighbors.

On these trips to my grandparents' farm, I often played with the children of the Czech workers who came to Lassee to help gather the harvest. I remember lining them up in the courtyard and teaching them to play such games as hopscotch, ring-around-the-rosy, and hide and go seek. The language barrier did not bother us.

These children tried to teach me a few Czech words, but I found the pronunciation very difficult because their words have so few vowels.

I wanted to go swimming with the farmers' children, but grandfather did not allow that. He also did not let me learn to ride his horses, but he was more lenient concerning his cows. I tried to learn to milk them but could never squeeze their tits hard enough or properly and nothing came out. I enjoyed being on the farm for weekends. The only things I really disliked was the drinking water which was very yellow, but safe to drink. I also resented that Uncle Rudi used to say that I was a spoiled little girl.

By the standards of Lassee, Grandpa Adolf Kohn was considered a very wealthy farmer. At my grandfather's funeral in 1930, when I was nine, the entire town turned out in a procession. There were wagons filled with flowers behind his coffin in the hearse, but they had to turn back at the railroad station since my grandfather was an Orthodox Jew and they do not accept flowers at funerals.

The villagers all knew that and respected it, in honor of my grandfather. Jewish children were shielded from death, so I stayed in grandfather's house with Mitzi, while everyone else went to Marchegg to attend the funeral. Control of the farm passed to Mutti's youngest brother Rudi. Her older brother Karl had died leaving an heir his young son Walter. Unfortunately, no express provisions had been made for Mutti and her sister Camilla to claim part of Grandpa Kohn's estate, resulting in a lawsuit among the three surviving adult siblings that dragged on for many many years.

The plenty one brings home from a farm does not extend to the clothes closet. To shore up our resources in this department, Mutti found the hope chest that Grandma Kohn had once prepared for her, and enlisted a dressmaker in our building to transform the unused, but outdated, dresses and coats into clothing for me, my cousins and some friends.

In Vienna, all Catholic holidays were celebrated by the entire city as state holidays. In 1931, when I was ten, Halloween was the subject of a school art assignment. I was always good at drawing and painting and I did a watercolor picture of what Halloween represented to me.

Halloween was celebrated at the cemeteries, as it was All Saints and All Souls Day. The huge Central Cemetery was the most interesting. It was walled and the statuary of the graves peeked over the wall. Large Angels and crosses, all kinds of tombstones with inscriptions were on the graves of the rich and famous. Brahms, Beethoven, Gluck, Franz Werfel, Johann Strauss, Schuhmann and Schubert among others were buried there. I was particularly fascinated when our maids (or my nanny) had taken me there to visit and walk in the procession with lit lanterns and flowers.

At the entrance against the wall were rows of flower stands, where women wearing babushkas sold wreaths of fall flowers and lanterns under their umbrellas. After purchasing such items, visitors walked in unison to the graves. My Halloween painting showed the cemetery wall with the various large angels and crosses behind the flower ladies. Then a thought occurred to me; I am Jewish. So I put a large star of David (the Jewish star) on top of each tombstone, angel and all the crosses. My painting was chosen to be in a special art exhibit. I suppose the judges had a sense of humor. At that time people were very liberal. The Social Democrats dominated Vienna then. It was known as "red Vienna", in contrast to the rest of the country of staunch Christian Socialists and some Nazis.

Besides being antique storeowners, my parents considered themselves part of Vienna's *Intelligencia.* My father was quite active in the Social Democratic party. I don't recall a time when my friends and I were not politically aware. We attended summer camps run by the Social Democrats. We sang political songs and marched in parades. Along with school, dance and piano lessons, political activities filled my childhood.

Political rivalries sometimes spilled into the schools at the elementary and high school level. Sometimes children of parents with different political affiliations would be made the captain of the playground team. They would choose children for this by their affiliations or religion rather than by their talent. I was very good at sports, but often I was not among the chosen students, which hurt me deeply.

A number of my classmates belonged to underground Nazi organizations. On occasions like big rallies or assemblies, where we were supposed to sing the Austrian national anthem, they substituted the words from the German national anthem, which had the same tune. Everyone understood how volatile the times were. In grammar school, part of our training in our gym class was how to extinguish incendiary bombs.

Papa always admonished me to speak softly, wear clothing that did not call out for attention, and wear no jewelry other than a watch. Because we were Jews, we were to try to blend into the crowd, not to stand out. Our home was located in Vienna's fourth district, an area of embassies and palaces, where only few Jewish families lived. Most Jews lived in Vienna's second district, a self-imposed ghetto. In all there were 21 districts in the city.

What a tumultuous year 1934 was, the year of my fourth year in the Gymnasium! Gymnasium was an eight-year High school that children attended from age ten on. Each of the main political parties had its own militia, with tension among them reaching a boiling point after Chancellor Engelbert Dollfuss, a Christian Socialist, dissolved the Parliament. On Feb. twelve, 1934, fighting broke out in the streets of Vienna. I remember my family being huddled in our kitchen for three days without electricity or water, while hearing the shooting all around us. We surreptitiously listened for news on Papa's crystal set radio, even though it was illegal to hear foreign broadcasts. I must admit that for me, staying at home with my parents and breaking radio rules was a great adventure. I was just a thirteen-year-old with little concept of the seriousness of the situation; I reveled in the fact that there was no school.

In response to the riots, Dollfuss abolished all political parties, except for one he decided to create, the Fatherland Front. The Nazis, however, would not have anyone stealing their thunder. On July 25, a small group of them seized the chancellery and assassinated Dollfuss. But instead of igniting a popular uprising, they were themselves seized and subsequently executed. In Germany, Hitler pretended that the Austrian Nazis had acted upon their own, and disavowed the plotters. In the wake of all this, Kurt von Schuschnigg, another Christian Socialist became Chancellor.

Not surprisingly in Vienna, the city of Theodor Herzl, there were numbers of Jews with Zionist sympathies, including my father's sister Adele and husband, Max. They decided in 1934 to emigrate to Palestine with their son Fritz. My parents purchased their textile business but even so, the decision was a financially difficult one for them. Austria did not permit any currency to be taken out of the country, and as a result Max and Adele lost two-thirds of their fortune. However, they were able to get enough money out of the country illegally to open an antique store in Haifa and to build an apartment building there.

With riots, an assassination and executions making headlines back then, it's hard to realize that life's ordinary rhythms also were occurring. For example, the landlord's handsome son Paul had just started to work as a law clerk in his father's office. The boys and girls who were my friends were close to my age, while Paul, still my idol, was at least 26. Sometimes, when Paul saw me walking down the *Favoriten Strasse* leading to the opera house, or if I were on the way to school, he would give me a ride in his car.

When I was fifteen, in 1936, I joined a social club by lying about my age. I told them that I was eighteen. Always well fed as a result of my connections to the farm in Lassee, I was larger than many of the boys, who seemed to have suffered from chronic undernourishment. While I socialized with the young men in the club, I still carried a torch for Paul, who thought of me, I suppose, as a little confidante. When he wanted to marry a girl named Toni, but his father wanted him to marry Mina, who was from a wealthy family. When he told me of his unhappiness. I protested that he must not marry Mina, but instead should follow the instincts of his heart. But his parents' insistence was more persuasive, and he married Mina. I received an invitation to his wedding in 1937 at the Hotel Bristol.

After the Anschluss

Hitler, meanwhile, kept up his pressure on Austria to come into the German Nazi orbit. He wanted to annex Austria, which is called "Anschluss." He successfully bullied our chancellor Schuschnigg into appointing a Nazi henchman, Arthur Seyss-Inquart, as the Minister of the Interior. My father, who had been president of many trade and other organizations, began receiving letter after letter removing him from his honorary jobs. Matters came to a head in 1938 when Kurt von Schuschnigg attempted to assert some measure of independence from Hitler. He announced that there would be a plebiscite on March 13 to determine whether Austria should remain independent or merge with Germany. Hitler, surprised by this announcement, did not want to take any chances.

Vienna, Austria March 11th 1938
My parents and I sat by our radio to listen to our chancellor. The radio announcer said as usual: "Hallo, Hallo, hier Radio Wien" then the voice of Kurt von Schuschnigg:.

Dr von Schuschnigg's last speech, broadcast at 7.30 p.m.
on Friday March 11th, 1938.

Austrian men Austrian women! This day has placed us
in a tragic and decisive situation. I have to give my Austrian
fellow countrymen the details of the events of the day.

The German Government handed today to President
Miklas an ultimatum, with a time-limit attached,
ordering him to nominate as Chancellor a person to be
designated by the German Government and to appoint
members of a cabinet on the orders of the German
Government; otherwise, German troops would invade
Austria.

I declare before the world that the reports issued in
Austria concerning disorders created by the workers and
the shedding of streams of blood and the allegation
that the situation had got out of the control of the

-2-

government were lies from A. To Z.

President Miklas asks me to tell the people of Austria that we have yielded to force, since we are not prepared in this terrible situation to shed blood, and we decided to order the troops to offer no serious – to offer no resistance.

The Inspector-General of the army, General Schilhaesly has been placed in command of the troops. He will issue further orders to them.

So I will take leave of the Austrian people with the German word of farewell, uttered from the depths of my heart, "GOD PROTECT AUSTRIA".

And that was the beginning. – –

The beginning of the end for some, the beginning of a new life for others, a new, more exciting and more adventurous life. And so for me, too I think. I mean the new, so very different life.

I translated and wrote the above speech when I was in England August 1938

H.P.

His troops crossed the border into Austria on March twelve, and he decreed *Anschluss* on March fourteen. A month later, under Nazi auspices, a plebiscite was held, and hardly anyone dared vote against it. With Nazi banners hanging from every public building, it was a *fait accompli*.

Jews immediately were subjected to a range of discriminatory laws and sudden arrests. We heard from his grandparents that my dear friend Paul had been sent to the Dachau concentration camp; we all cried and cried. Nevertheless, my father was in a state of denial. Although he received an avalanche of letters from trade organizations, relieving him not only of his offices, but also of his memberships, he continued to believe that the situation would calm down; that Hitler could not get away with his monstrous and outrageous policies. It would all blow over, we should lay low and ride it out.

However, new edicts continued to be posted. Jews were not allowed to continue university studies, nor stay in other schools of higher learning. We were forbidden to sit on park benches, or to enter certain shops, and were constrained by many other rules, too numerous to mention. One night, there was a pounding on our door, and when Papa opened it, he was confronted by seven men in Nazi uniforms. These SS and SA men forced Papa to sit at his desk and sign all kinds of papers, "voluntarily" donating his antique furniture store, his warehouse and all its contents, to Nazi hands. Our bank accounts were frozen—and money from Grandpa Kohn's estate that my mother finally had won in the lawsuit—were required to be paid into a *Sperrkonto,* or blocked account. I pleaded with Papa not to sign the Nazi documents—"Papa, don't do it, don't sign anything," I begged—but Mutti dragged me out of the room and pleaded with me to keep still lest it cost us our lives. The thugs left with all the keys and papers, all our valuable possessions, antique furniture, bankbooks and all the business books. A Nazi manager took over the antique store and its warehouses, with Papa required to remain one month to train him how to run it.

We were stunned, numb, and in shock. But we were alive and, at least, we did not share the fate of Paul and many others, who were sent to Dachau. This incident did at least serve one salutary purpose. It persuaded Papa that we should do what we could to get out of Austria. He wrote to his sister, Adele, in Haifa, and to his brother, Nathan, in Alexandria, Egypt, asking for help. Although this was a year before Britain issued its White paper, closing off immigration to Palestine to mollify Arab interests, even then it was practically impossible to enter Palestine—unless you could prove that you had a large amount of money to bring with you. If you had, you could obtain the equivalent of a "capitalist" visa. Since we were robbed by the Nazis of our capital, we could no longer qualify.

Without telling my parents I made the rounds of foreign Embassies and Consulates to inquire about immigration to their countries. The only country I could find that was willing to accept immigrants without regulations or difficulties was Liberia, in West Africa. My heart was set on getting to the United States. But before I could even hope to do that, I needed to locate some American citizen who would be willing to sponsor us. This was no small commitment. A sponsor had to agree to be responsible for the support of the immigrants for up to five years, unless they were able to become self-sufficient before then.

How nice it would have been to have a proverbial rich uncle in the United States, but we had no such relative. Perhaps, I thought, I could find someone who felt a connection to us because they had the same name. In the offices of the U.S. Consulate, I found telephone books for major American cities. I discovered a Lou Harmel listed in New York City, and Paul Harmels in both Washington D.C., and Cleveland. Using a German-English dictionary, which showed how the word you looked up is used in a sentence, I wrote a letter to each of these gentlemen, enclosing my photograph. The following letter was written when I was sixteen years old.

Vienna, May sixteenth 1938

Dear Sir,

My name is Harmel like yours. I am a sixteen year old Viennese Jewish girl, tall and healthy. Unfortunately, in consequence of the changed circumstances, I am forced to emigrate. My father, (merchant in Vienna) often told me of an uncle who had gone to America many years ago. My parents and I are now in a very bad situation.

We got your address by chance and knew of no other way as to write this letter. I hope to God to find in you our relative or if that is not the case, our kindhearted helper. I ask you urgently not to throw this letter into the paper basket and if it is not possible for you, to forward my request to some of your friends, who might be able to help us. I built all of my hopes upon this letter. I beg of you to answer. I was born in Vienna as an Austrian citizen, am now German and am Jewish. I passed four years grammar school, four years Gymnasium (High School) and one year Commerce Academy. I am a good cook, can manicure and hair dressing for ladies and am able to do all domestic works. I speak English, French, Italian and German, my mother tongue. I am sure if I had the possibility to leave this country, that I shall not be a burden to anybody. What I need is an affidavit.

This would only be a formality for I do not want any money from you and I am really willing to work. Neither do I want any financial help for the journey and I am of course ready to return the costs which you might have, to get an affidavit. Will you pardon please my impudence. I should never have dared to come up with such a request if the Americans were not famous for their magnanimity and if our distress were not so great. I am expecting your answer with impatience and remain with best thanks in advance and kind regards,

Yours gratefully,

Hilda Harmel

P.S. I shall bring clothes for some years and enclose my picture

About this time, we received a letter from Uncle Nathan in Alexandria advising us not to leave Austria but to stick it out. My parents, he thought, were too old and set in their ways to adjust to a new country, and Egypt was not a place where we could be happy. Even the climate would not be right for us, he advised. While he had been living with his wife, Duja, in Egypt, they had lost two sons as a result of drinking unpasteurized milk. That had prompted Duja and her daughter, Lilian, to move to Vienna approximately in 1908. Aunt Duja operated a pension, a large apartment with rooms to rent. Because she retained her status as a British subject, Aunt Duja, Lilian and her husband Dr. Lothar Rubinstein were able to escape the Nazis by moving to England.

My Aunt Adele wrote from Haifa that she would try to help us.

And then a miracle happened—a letter arrived from the Lou Harmels in New York City saying they were hoping that I would come to live with them. They said they had two sons slightly older than me, who were away at college. Their family had roots in Russia, not in Poland like my father's family, so it was unlikely we were related. Nevertheless, they said they were in the process of making arrangements to get proper papers for my entry to the USA. We were thrilled.

Next, only a few days later, a letter arrived from Chicago. It was from the daughter and son-in-law of the Paul Harmels in Washington, D.C., from whom they had received a copy of my letter. Mr. and Mrs. B.B. Schneider of Chicago wrote that they had a daughter, Maxine, who was my age, who could become a ready-made sister to me. Furthermore, Mr. Schneider was himself a patent attorney and was preparing the documents for me to come to the United States.

Our joy was boundless. We immediately conveyed our thanks and began to make plans. As it turned out the Harmels of Washington, New York and Cleveland were all related. After they realized I had written to each of them, they decided that Cleveland was not a good choice for me because the Paul Harmel there was a young attorney caring for a sick mother. The Harmels provided me with the requested affidavits, and recommended that I eventually come to live with either family in New York or Chicago.

The affidavits were only the first steps in the process towards obtaining a visa from the United States government. I learned that the United States had a quota, and that I must wait until my quota number was reached. Meanwhile conditions continued to worsen for Jews in Vienna. Mutti and I were attacked while walking on the street, and forced to scrub swastika symbols off the sidewalks with toothbrushes. They poured a sharp liquid over our hands and it burned terribly. While we were on our hands and knees scrubbing, onlookers threw rocks at us, screamed invectives, spat upon us and kicked us. .

How we ever got back home I don't even recall. Papa helped wash us and put us to bed. He did not ask us what had happened and we could not say anything, because we were numb. Papa did not go to the store anymore and had to hide. Most of the time he did not leave the apartment at all. Our household help left us. Our neighbors, whom we had known all our lives and thought were good friends, did not speak to us anymore. My classmates spat on me when they passed by. So did neighbor children with whom I had grown up, making crossing the garden of our building complex a gauntlet to run. Going to buy food became very risky. The green grocer, the butcher, the baker, the laundry people, all of whom our family had known for a lifetime, refused to wait on us until after every other customer was taken care of. And then, they just threw the stuff at us. These were the same people, to whom we had brought food when there was almost none; whose children had come to eat with us; and who had purchased furniture from us on credit and now did not pay us.

Grandmother Therese came to live in Vienna with Aunt Camilla after Uncle Rudi was forced to turn the farm over to the Nazis in 1938. Rudi left for Uruguay with his wife and daughter. My cousin Benno, one year older than I, was able to join his paternal uncle in London. Eventually his parents traveled to New York, where Benno subsequently joined them. My cousin Erich and his wife Ellen tried to escape illegally by walking across the mountains into Switzerland, but were turned back. But somehow they managed to get to New York eventually.

We started to hear rumors about atrocities committed against the Jews at Dachau and other camps, but we did not believe them. Families of camp inmates received shoeboxes with ashes, supposedly of their loved ones. How could a rational person believe such horrendous things?

Adjacent to our building was what once had been a large, blank wall. The Nazis covered it with posters bearing enlarged cartoons from the newspaper, *Der Stuermer*. These were foul, horrible caricatures of Jews as dogs and moneylenders. The entire city of Vienna was draped with thousands of red flags bearing the huge swastika. In Germany, Field Marshall Goering coined the phrase: *"Wir brauchen keine Butter, wir brauchen Kanonen."* We do not need butter; we need cannons.

Germans rerouted traffic, requiring drivers to now keep to the right side of the street instead of the left. Because people had difficulty adjusting to this over-night, there were many accidents, it was bedlam. Austria's premium foodstuffs were shipped to Germany to provide them with luxury foods they did not have. Whipping cream, once a staple in our coffee, disappeared from the stores as did butter, meats, silks, art and other luxury items.

From America came wonderful letters. Maxine Schneider wrote she could hardly wait to meet her new "sister," while the two New York Harmel college boys wrote from Ann Arbor and Johns Hopkins University and sent photos. Yet, April, May, June, July all passed without word from the American Consulate about my visa. We constantly wrote for help to the Harmels in New York and the Schneiders in Chicago, urging them to plead with the U.S. State Department to hurry things up. Although they tried hard, their efforts were unsuccessful.

We finally heard from my aunt in Haifa, who said she was going to Cyprus to try to get permission for my parents to go there while waiting for Palestine entry permits. She said it would take some time. Meanwhile, she had been in touch with my Uncle Nathan in Alexandria and had persuaded him to join forces with her in Cyprus

In the meantime on several occasions I tried to get inside the U.S. Consulate, waiting in line as long as eleven hours. By the time I finally got to the door, it was closing time. I wanted to go at midnight to start my wait, thereby guaranteeing a spot in front of the line, but my parents would not permit me to do so. It was terribly dangerous. To make good use of this period of waiting, I started taking English lessons, attended a famous culinary school, and went for lessons at a millinery shop.

Notwithstanding my parents' wishes, I snuck out of the house, on a rainy Monday morning, while it still was dark and raining outside. I was armed with my umbrella. I ran for 20 minutes to get to the U.S. Consulate, hugging the walls of buildings as I went.

This time, the line of people was shorter. My chance to get in was good. An older couple in front of me had brought stools to sit on. They had been there for many hours and were wet through and through. We exchanged stories. Their eighteen-year-old son had been arrested but still was somewhere in Vienna, and they hoped to get him out in time to go to America with them. The mother declared she would not leave without her son. I felt so sorry for them.

The rain did not let up. My feet were soaked. I was shivering, but it was getting light and ten or more people were behind me in line. At least the rain kept the hecklers away. I calculated that by noon we would be able to get inside. As the downpour became more intense, we stopped talking; so miserable and chilled did we feel. My feet felt numb and I tried walking in place. I ate the roll that I had in my pocket.

Finally the line started moving forwards slowly and it was getting warmer. As my raincoat was not waterproof, my back was soaked through. My pageboy hairdo was a mess. The line had finally turned the corner and I could now see the large entrance of the building. At this point, a huge black limousine with an American flag on the hood pulled up to the door. Several men and a woman got out as a uniformed doorman held a large umbrella to shield them from the torrential rain.

I broke out of line, ran to the door, and pushed my way into the foyer while the doorman tried to close his umbrella and run after me. I don't know how I found the strength and courage, but I ran up the broad staircase and through the first door into a large room, through another door, and fell into a chair totally out of breath. My heart felt like it was beating in my mouth. It seemed so loud, I was afraid someone might hear it and find me. The room was dark, the blinds were drawn. There was a big desk and a sofa. The chair on which I was sitting had become wet from my dripping clothes. I didn't have my umbrella anymore, and my shoes were making puddles on the parquet floor.

When the door opened, a lady said something to me in English. I responded, "My name is Hilda Harmel and I need to speak to the American Consul." I had practiced that speech at home. Then, breaking into German, I told her that I had two affidavits and I needed to get out of Vienna right away because my parents were going to Cyprus, and I could not be left behind alone. I would throw myself into the waters of the Danube, to kill myself, if I could not go to America. Tears were streaming down my already wet face.

She motioned to me to stay where I was and she left the room, returning with a glass of water. What a blessing. I was very thirsty. I assumed that she had understood the word "water" when I spoke of the Danube. At that moment, a very tall, elegant gentleman came in and sat down at the desk. "All right, young lady, why are you here?" In my purse were the letters I had from America. Mr. Wiley, the chief consul of the United States in Vienna, read them carefully. He made some phone calls, and then an employee brought a file. "You have affidavits indeed," the kindly Mr. Wiley said at last. "But you have to wait for your quota number and that will take some time ."I understood the word "time" and I had none of it. "No time," I protested, crying anew. He shook his head and handed me his handkerchief. "No time! No time!" I kept repeating.

He referred me to a man who he said might help me. He urged me to write to this man, who was coming to Vienna from New York. I was advised to write to Alfred Jaretzky in care of him, John Wiley, at the American Consulate in Vienna. He handed me the paper, got up, shook my hand, ushered me to the door, and pointed to the stairway. I thanked him and the lady and curtsied Viennese style. He told me to keep the hanky.

I ran home and burst in on Mutti cooking lunch and Papa listening to the radio. "Stop what you are doing, I have so much to tell you!" I said. My voice was agitated. I pulled off my wet coat, sank into a chair and pulled off my shoes, while relating the day's events to them, as they sat spellbound.

We promptly retrieved our dictionary and Papa helped me write a letter to Mr. Jaretzky.

In only two days, we received a telephone call from an Embassy secretary asking me to come to the Hotel Bristol to meet Mr. Jaretzky that very afternoon. My mother did not think it was proper for me to meet a strange man in a hotel room. He might be a white slaver and sell me to a brothel in South America. Papa and I calmed her down by convincing her that a friend of the American Consul in Vienna would not conspire to such an undertaking.

Unconvinced, Mutti called the *Kultus Gemeinde*, the Jewish Agency, which supported synagogues with the taxes collected from members of the Jewish community of Vienna. They indeed knew of Mr. Jaretzky, who was in Europe at the behest of the American Joint Distribution Committee, an important American Jewish charity. I insisted therefore on going alone; it was too risky for all three of us to be on the street together.

In my best black skirt, lilac silk blouse, my mother's patent leather shoes and handbag, I walked all the way to the Hotel Bristol, opposite the Vienna State Opera House. I had been there the previous year for Paul's wedding. A doorman directed me to the information desk. He gave me Mr. Jaretzky's room number and I took the glass elevator to the third floor.

I found Mr. Jaretzky and a young woman in the sitting room. He got up to greet me and invited me to sit down. The lady was Viennese and in German I told my story which she translated. Mr. Jaretzky said he could not speed up the visa process, it might take a year or more for the visa to come through because I had a high quota number. This caused me considerable frustration because I remembered having urged Papa to apply earlier for a quota number. Papa had resisted because he thought it foolish to go through the required submittals of tax records, bank statements and other official papers when it seemed unlikely we would have any chance to go to America. By the time I obtained the affidavits from the American Harmels, many other people had filed applications.

Miss Harmel, I can help you get out of Austria, for you to wait for your visa in safety, either in Brussels, Belgium, or London, England," Mr. Jaretzky told me. "Go home, confer with your parents, come back tomorrow and I will make the necessary arrangements."

I had my heart set on going to America but his alternatives were a way out of this hellish situation in my beloved home country. My parents agreed. Papa thought Brussels would be good, since I could learn French there. "No way do I want to come to America like a mute," I responded. "England is the country I will go to." We talked until dawn, and by nine in the morning I was back at the Hotel Bristol.

A different woman was there with Mr. Jaretzky, Miss Ruth Fellner from London. "We have very little time," she translated for Mr. Jaretzky. "You need an English transit visa. Do you have all your exit permits from the Austrian government?" I was happy to be able to say "yes," I had obtained them just the week before. It had taken weeks of standing in long lines, and considerable paper work to get the documents from many different government offices. Now he told me to take a taxi home, gather up all my documents and meet him at the British Embassy at two p.m. He also asked whether my parents had enough money to purchase a ticket for me on the French liner, *Normandy,* from London to New York with the departure date left open. Also, my father should give a donation to the Jewish Children's Refugee Committee in London, who would help me in England with pocket money.

I told him that I would ask my father, but believed that it was possible. Mr. Jaretzky then gave me the surprise of my life: "I am leaving for London tomorrow August fifteenth (1938) on a flight at eleven in the morning and will take you with me. I hope you can manage to get a ticket on the same flight. While you and I get your British visa, your parents need to book your passage to New York and the flight for tomorrow. You, young lady, need to pack your things." My head was spinning. Did Miss Fellner translate properly? Did he really think I could get a visa for England so fast and really leave with him the next day? Three times I asked if I really understood it all correctly. Both of them smiled and said it was so.

The doorman called a taxi for me. In ten minutes I was home, spilling out all the tasks before us and getting all my important papers together. Papa said the money was no object. Mutti cried a lot, but got the suitcases out for packing. Papa took money from a hiding place (thank goodness the Gestapo had not found it) and left for the shipping line, which was within walking distance of our apartment. I hoped that he had sufficient money for himself and Mutti to depart. Papa booked me to London via Prague.

I arrived at the British Embassy on time with all my papers in hand. Mr. Jaretzky and I went to the visa division and in ten minutes I had a three-month transit visa in my passport. It seemed like an impossible dream. I wanted to kiss the hand of my benefactor, but he gave me a hug and said, "tomorrow at Aspern Flughof for our eleven o'clock flight."

There were seven suitcases standing in our entry hall. In a nice red leather case were my tickets for the flight as well as for my first-class passage on the *Normandy,* the star of the French Line fleet. None of us slept that night. We decided that there were not going to be any tears. We told ourselves this was a happy occasion and that we were going to be reunited, somehow, somewhere, some time.

We concocted a code for letter writing because all mail was strictly censored. Laundry would mean money and jewelry, neighbor meant grandmother, uncle meant Nazis, tired meant hungry. Schloss meant apartment. It was not a very clever code but we had neither time nor peace of mind to think too clearly.

The next morning, all three of us left for the airport, with all the luggage squeezed into the taxi.

The two-propeller Czech plane, just like one that had crashed the day before, was sitting on the runway. Never having been on an airplane before it was most exciting for me. Mr. Jaretzky came over to us and told my parents not to worry. He told us that Miss Fellner would be waiting in London and take good care of me. He said that I was a fine young woman and would look after myself, and that they should be proud of me and not have to worry.

Papa and Mutti thanked him profusely. They kissed me wordlessly, no tears, no admonishments. They just stood there … as I boarded the plane and took a seat by the window. I waved to them as the plane took off and saw them getting smaller and smaller until I could not see them any more because of the clouds.

Then there was the Danube, the Vienna Woods, and a last glimpse of Vienna below us.

Of course I was fully aware that I might never see my parents again, but my eyes stayed dry. The experience of seeing my familiar world from a new angle was new and impressive, and, besides, I felt numb. Mr. Jaretzky was reading. It was fine with me that we did not converse. After landing in Prague, we had lunch in a nice airport restaurant and I found a postcard to send back home.

When we landed in London, the Immigration officials refused to accept my visa. Without Mr. Jaretzky, they would have sent me back. It took several hours for Mr. Jaretzky to straighten things out and for them to let me enter. It was very upsetting to me that my kind benefactor was delayed so long on my account. We took a taxi and headed for Claridge's, an elegant hotel in London.

London

My traveling wardrobe, assembled by Mutti, included seven evening gowns because we had heard that English and American families dressed for dinner, and we thought this meant formals. In my mind, I chose the green one to wear for dinner at Claridge's.

We were greeted in the lobby by Miss Fellner who, after greetings and explanations, packed me off into a taxi. She deposited me in a small boarding house in Swiss Cottage and told me to come to Woburn House the next morning to discuss her plans for me.

I had only five dollars worth of Austrian schillings with me—all that I was permitted to take out of Austria. I had no idea where I could change it into English money for bus fare.

A woman at the boardinghouse showed me to my tiny little room on the second floor. She helped me drag my seven suitcases upstairs. It was too late for dinner there, so I spent my first night in England hungry. In fact, I was so drained from the long and traumatic day that I fell asleep right away.

I heard the gong calling for breakfast. Gathered around the large table were ten people of many different nationalities. One man spoke German and told me that the funny tasting coffee was not coffee at all, but tea with milk. He also told me that a block or so from the boarding house was a bank where I could change money and that close by was an Underground station where I could get a train to Woburn Place.

Ruth Fellner was overwhelmed with work since so many refugee children had arrived who needed housing. She had made arrangements for me to go to the Society of Friends (Quakers) who would find a place for me. She gave me a little money and the address of the Quakers' office. There, a social worker said they had found a position for me to train as a children's nurse in the Lady Cynthia Moseley Day Nursery in Kennington Oval, a slum area in London. It would take two or three weeks to finalize the arrangements and I should stay where I was until then.

It sounded good to me. Breakfast and dinner were provided at my lodgings. For lunch I bought some apples, which I kept in my room. The arrangement left me free to explore London. My Uncle Nathan's daughter, Lilian, and her husband, Dr. Lothar Rubinstein, a psychiatrist, had preceded me to London by three months and I could visit them.

Lothar was writing a book with Anna Freud. He told me that her father, Sigmund Freud, and Anna lived next door to my boarding house. He promised to introduce me to them. At that stage of his life the famous interpreter of dreams was very frail, and had cancer of the mouth. He took a walk on the arm of his daughter every day. After I was introduced to the Freuds, I saw them every day for the three weeks that I lived in the boarding house. He always said "good morning" or "good afternoon, Fraulein Hilda," even though he had difficulty speaking.

I wrote to my parents daily. Most of my time I spent at the National Gallery of Art, the British Museum and the Tate Gallery. Entry was free and I felt at home with the paintings because I had become familiar with the same great artists in the Viennese museums. Ever since I was old enough to walk, my parents took me to museums on winter Sundays.

This was the hottest London summer in many years, but the galleries were nice and cool. My daily destination was a bench facing the painting by Andrea del Sarto of a young man with a beret. The longer I sat there, the more he seemed to look at me. I mentally talked to him, since there was no one else I could talk to.

I was contacted in London by Paul's sister Trude, the granddaughter of our old landlord in Vienna. She came to see me to pick up a letter her father had given me to carry from Vienna. I assumed it was an important letter of some sort, but instead it turned out to be a letter of credit for a huge amount of money. My first reaction was fury. If the Gestapo had stopped me with such a letter before I left Vienna, my life would have been finished. How could Paul's father, a lawyer, have put me into such terrible danger?

However, I had some compensating news that lifted my spirits. Trude told me that her brother, my idol, Paul, was alive! After he had been sent to Dachau, his wealthy wife, Mina, set about with admirable determination, to win his release. One of the girls who had been her classmate at a finishing school in Switzerland was the daughter of Hermann Goering, Hitler's field marshal. Mina, a brave soul, put her own life at risk by contacting Fraulein Goering and asking her to please speak to her father about releasing Paul. The daughter persuaded the field marshal to see Trude and Mina in his office in Berlin. Dressed in their best clothes, they pleaded Paul's case. Goering said: "By the time your train returns to Vienna, Paul would be released." And for once, a Nazi was true to his word. In Dachau, the guards had broken Paul's hip. Trude said that he now walked with a limp. But, oh, what difference did that make? He was alive!

After three weeks, I took my position at the day nursery. Some letters I wrote in dictionary English to the Schneider family in Chicago conveyed the situation:

September 1st 1938 London

Dear Mr. and Mrs. Schneider and Dearest Maxine,

I am now a student in the Lady Cynthia Moseley Day Nursery. But never in my life have I heard that students have to do work like I have to do here. I must besides nursing the children, scrub the unfinished wood furniture and the floor with Lysol. Do the laundry and wash dirty diapers by hand also with Lysol. And work I do not want to describe from 6:30 in the morning until 8:30 at night. For that hard work I must pay one English pound per month for training. I wear a uniform with a stiff collar and cap and I am not able to rest for one minute the whole week. I should not mind the work but another German Jewish girl and I have to feel very hard that we are strangers, Jews, without money, without parents, without any assistance. Unfortunately, they are here as anti-Semitic as in Germany. The difference is only that here they do not say it. My friend May and I are here very unhappy. We do our best to let them know that also Jewish girls can do hard and dirty work without making a fuss and we do not show them that we are tired on the evening to fall down. In spite of these I am very happy to be in England as I have now only half the way to you. One week ago I got information from the American Consulate in London that I have to come with all my papers on the 7th of October 1938 to the Consulate and I'll get the visa after 4 months. I am therefore the happiest girl of the whole world. Only this letter let me stand the situation here, oh how I hate the English! They hardly speak a word a day with me. I have only the children. They are the very sweet and the only people in England being kind with me. I hope to be soon able to thank you very much personally for all your kindness, I remain with kindest regards,

Yours gratefully,

Hilda

Three days after I wrote that letter, British Prime Minister Neville Chamberlain delivered his infamous "peace in our time" speech in the House of Commons. He was attempting to justify his willingness at the Munich Conference to let Hitler gobble up Czechoslovakia.

There were many people in Britain who admired Hitler. The Matron at the Day Nursery had told me that she thought Hitler was a great man, and that the Jews deserved to be gotten rid of—especially a useless girl like me. That inspired me to study my English dictionary every night in bed, just so I could tell her what I thought of her and her training program. As I toiled at my jobs, I thought with grim satisfaction how wrong Uncle Rudi had been about me. It was not the work; it was the lack of respect and their hostility toward Jews that made the situation intolerable. I simply had to leave there. I squeezed myself out of a tiny bathroom window, ran across the street to a green grocer, gave him my little diamond ring as collateral for carfare for me to go to Woburn House and see Miss Fellner. He understood I'd want my ring back when I gave him back the money.

I told Miss Fellner about the conditions at the Nursery. I said I'd rather go back to Vienna and be with my parents, come what may. She was not pleased about the situation, but she permitted me to go back to tell the Matron I had permission to leave there. Which I did. The Matron said a lot of nasty things to me, most of which, luckily, I did not understand. I said not a word. I went to my room and packed all my luggage and left the hated uniform in the room.

Later I learned that Cynthia Moseley (after whom the school was named) was the deceased wife of Sir Oswald Moseley—the openly pro-Nazi member of the House of Lords, who had aspirations to be the English Hitler. Learning this, I was shocked that a better job of screening had not been done by the Jewish Agency. I'm sure the Agency didn't want to subject us to such horrible people anymore than we relished being with the likes of the Moseleys. As for "peace in our time," within a short time after Chamberlain's speech, the authorities were handing out gas masks to civilians, including me.

My spirits were low, but not so low as those of other European girls caught in similar situations. Under Britain's laws, the only work available to us immigrants was that of domestics, no matter what our other skills were. Exploitation under such circumstances was not uncommon. One day, by chance, I met Susie, a girl who had attended the same school as I did in Vienna. She was one year older than I. She told me that she had been mistreated while working as a maid in an English household, and had run away. She ran away in a desperate moment and found men on the street with whom she had sex for money. She said she could now afford a nice room in a little hotel and good food and clothes. She offered to teach me how to do the same. I was shocked, of course. I tried to talk her out of her life as a prostitute. That was not the thing for a girl from a fine Jewish family in Vienna to be doing. But she and I just left each other and continued in different directions

---

September 19th 1938

Dearest Maxine,

I am the happiest girl in Europe. I left the Nursery. I could not stay there for all the world. I am now in a room in a boarding house and tomorrow I shall know if I shall go to school or learn millinery or something else. I shall do all they tell me. Now I feel that I am in a free country and I know that the sun is shining for me as well as for the others. Only the specter of war is in everybody's thoughts. It is here a terrible tension. Through a trick I was able to leave the Nursery for two hours. I ran in my uniform to the Woburn House. Miss Fellner was not pleased with the situation but allowed me to tell the Matron at the Nursery that I was allowed to leave. Which I did.

I Embrace you with all my love,

Hilda

The Society of Quakers sent me to a foster family in Crawley Down, Sussex. I begged them to let me stay in London, where I had found an advertisement for a girl to work in a hat factory. The owners of the factory were Jewish. They had lost a daughter and when they heard my story, they not only immediately offered me a job, but also a home with them. When I told that to the social worker at the Quakers, she in turn called Miss Fellner. Both said it was impossible because I was too young to get a work permit. Even if I were old enough, England issued such permits only for domestic work.

With war threatening, Miss Fellner wanted me out of the city of London. I had tears in my eyes when I returned to the hat factory to tell them the turn of events. The kind family telephoned Miss Fellner and said they would like to adopt me. I told them that I had wonderful parents and did not want to be adopted. They said I could be their foster child because they had fallen in love with me. But Miss Fellner was adamant. Since she was in charge, I had to do her bidding. She insisted that I go to Crawley Down to live with a gentile family. I said a sad goodbye to the lovely couple, who was so nice to me.

I was very worried. What if this gentile couple felt the same way about Jews as the matron did? How would I be able to run away from a home in the countryside? I was afraid to go. Nevertheless, a social worker drove me to Crawley Down, Sussex, the next day.

The English Countryside

In England all houses have names, and that of my new residence was "Thorn Hedges." At the gate to a small garden, the Roseveare family greeted us. The family consisted of Major William Roseveare, Mrs. Marjory Roseveare, Brenda Roseveare, who was my age, and Barney, the friendly Springer Spaniel. The beautiful lady embraced and kissed me. Brenda gave me a hug. Barney jumped up on me and wagged his stubby tail. Major Roseveare gave me a big smile and grabbed two of my suitcases.

Brenda and I and the social worker carried the rest of my luggage up the steep stairway to what was going to be my room. I realized that there was no need for me to be afraid. I had found a good home.

My visa was expected to come through in three months and that was how long the Roseveares wanted me to stay with them. After that, their son Rob would need his room, when he got home from boarding school. It was a tiny room, but the Major showed me two little attic storerooms where my suitcases could go after I unpacked them.

I learned that he and his wife had been in Burma for the last seventeen years. There he served with the Royal Engineers as an expert in irrigation. Their children, like most English children of parents in the colonies, were sent to boarding school in England at age six or seven. They saw their parents only every two years for a visit. This was the Roseveare's first year back home as a family.

They told me to call them Auntie and Uncle and to give Brenda lessons in German in exchange for her teaching me English. She was to correct my grammar and to supervise my reading of English books and newspapers. Satisfied that all would go well, the Quakers' social worker left at this point. Brenda helped me unpack, and as the closets were very small, I had to leave a lot of my clothes in the suitcases. She suggested that I stow one suitcase packed with clothes I needed, under the bed. She also recommended that I find something silky to wear for dinner.

The dining room table was set with beautiful china, silver and crystal. Uncle Bill at the head of the table was doing the carving. My father never did that. Auntie Marjory had prepared a dinner with roast beef and Yorkshire pudding. There was also some very bitter type of mustard. In Vienna, I had never seen anything like the doughy pancake, runny in the middle, or the beef red and almost raw. I masked the difficulty I had swallowing it. For dessert came a suet pudding with treakle (a wet doughy lump, with a dark kind of bitter syrup). I had heard that English cuisine was very different from Viennese food, but I was unprepared for how different. While the food at the nursery in London had been generally awful, it was not strange.

Although the food took some getting used to, I felt comfortable with the Roseveare family immediately. They all were so lovely and kind. Of course I jumped up and helped clear the table and offered to help with washing the dishes.

We then went to the drawing room where Uncle Bill put a recording of "The Mikado" on the victrola. Gilbert and Sullivan were new to me. Brenda wanted to know what my apartment in Vienna was like and whether I had photos of my parents. I ran upstairs and brought down the picture we had taken before I left. I described our apartment in such longing detail, it brought tears to my eyes. Auntie Marjory comforted me with a kiss. "Sleep well and know that you are safe," she told me. "Someday you can go back there again."

Brenda gave me a copy of a book of fairy tales by the Brothers Grimm, and as the stories were so familiar to me, I easily could understand the writing. Brenda was a good teacher and introduced me to her many friends and cousins. In no time, I was chattering in English and driving people crazy with my questions. "How do you spell that word?" I asked frequently. I also learned that the English believed in keeping their emotions in check. "Keep a stiff upper lip," was a saying the Roseveares and their neighbors believed in. They were quite reserved, except Auntie Marjory. She was the most outgoing and warmest member of the family. She was so kind and also let me use her bike. She was a very unusually wonderful woman and I adored her.

The Roseveares took me to church services and everyone there seemed eager to meet me and asked me all kinds of questions about the situation in Austria. Most of them had never met a Jewish person. Some women asked if they could touch me, since I was the same kind of human as the Lord Jesus.

Correspondence from my parents, although in code, painted a horrifying picture of their situation. They had been forced to leave their apartment and to move into a coal cellar in a different building with several other Jewish families. Aunt Adele's efforts to get them an entry permit for Cyprus were unsuccessful. Stuck in Vienna, they feared daily they would be deported to a concentration camp. Uncle Bill Roseveare promised me he would make every effort he could to get an English visa for them. I had no idea that he had to deposit money with the English Home Office in order to sponsor their immigration. It took months before they could actually come to England, but in the meantime the Roseveares had been busy—as I found out over Christmas vacation.

As their son Rob would be coming home for the holidays, it was arranged for me to stay in the rectory in the village of Balsham, near Cambridge. It meant a trip by train and bus. I should experience life at the rectory, said the Roseveares, because there was the possibility that my parents could be given jobs there as domestics—the only employment allowed to immigrants. It was possible that my father would serve as a butler and my mother work as a cook when they could finally get to England.

Balsham, I discovered, was a village without electricity. Thatched-roof homes were lit with oil lamps and I felt myself transported back in time at least 100 years.

The rectory was a huge, stone mansion with eighteen bedrooms. The rector's family took in paying guests to help the rector, his wife and daughter defray their expenses. It was located next to a very large church, almost the size of a cathedral, and the adjacent cemetery. The church was built in the fourteenth century and the Rectory in 17 64. Rector Williams was a tall and slender Welshman, possibly in his sixties. He was very kind and very pleasant. I later surmised that he, nevertheless, was not well liked in this village because he was considered a foreigner from Wales, although he had been in England for over 30 years.

Mrs. Williams was bedridden with an illness that the family did not identify to me. Their twenty-seven-year-old daughter, Nancy, was very friendly and nice to me. I was given a huge bedroom overlooking the cemetery and the church. A garden the size of a large park surrounded the rectory. It had a pond and a gazebo and huge old trees. Tourists came to visit the famous old church. Sometimes they made rubbings of the old tombstones and plaques on the floor of the church.

There was almost no heat in the rectory at all. Only one fireplace in the living room was ever lit. I wore three layers of clothes to ward off freezing. The oil lamps gave off a very poor light. The dining room and living room had lamps attached to the wall, also a huge chandelier with oil lamps. One had to take a lit lamp to one's bedroom at night and a hot water bottle to put under the damp, cold bedding. The servants had to clean out all the smoky glass cylinders of the oil lamps, refill them with oil every morning and re-install them. It was hard work. The kitchen had an old fashioned coal stove. The winter of 1938 was unusually cold and snowy, even as the past summer had been unusually hot and sticky. We wore gloves inside the house.

I felt very sorry that my parents would to have to deal with that kind of household, but it certainly was a lot better than Vienna under Hitler! If only they were in England already.

The endless waiting was very difficult for all of us. Christmas in the rectory was quite wonderful. Rector Williams let me read and type up his sermons. He was a very compassionate man. But his church was poorly attended. The cavernous nave was freezing cold, damp and empty. I learned so much about the Church of England but he never tried or even intimated that he would like to convert me. I appreciated that. Nancy played the church organ, which had to be pumped. That was my job. Mrs. Williams, whom I could occasionally hear screeching and shouting commands had a special care giver.

Nancy showed me how to make and play bamboo flutes. Her friends invited us to many Christmas parties, where we played many enjoyable games. My experience there was enjoyable. In one game, we all were blindfolded, and someone held a tray of objects. We would touch an object and try to guess what it was. It was fun. So was singing Christmas carols and hymns.

After Christmas, cousins of the Roseveare family wanted me to stay with them while I still waited for the U.S visa which had not arrived. I also needed to fill out an application for renewal of my English transit visa. I understood that Brenda, after so many years of boarding school without her parents, needed some time alone with them.

I accepted the invitation from Mrs. Isobel Blaikie and her daughter Muriel, who had a lovely house in Copthorne, a short bike ride from Crawley Down. Another village close by was East Grinstead, where we did all the shopping. Auntie Marjory had taken me to the Blaikies for tea several times. Mrs. Blaikie seemed to be a very stern, unemotional lady. She had lost her son in the service of the British Empire and never spoke of him nor allowed anyone else to mention his name. But she was quite generous. She helped me obtain papers for my girlfriend, Lizzi Albrecht, to get out of Vienna and live with a family in Copthorne like me. The Blaikies gave me the largest and most beautiful bedroom overlooking that wonderful garden. Mrs. Blaikie was also a fine cook, and both she and Muriel were keen gardeners, so much so, that their garden was a show place. I learned the names of all the flowers that they so lovingly tended. The soil was so rich that it boasted many big fat worms, which made me shudder when I dug them up. I preferred cutting and arranging the flowers.

Although Muriel was sixteen years older than I, she was very child-like and fun. When she taught Sunday school at their strict, unornamented Scottish-rite church, I served as her assistant and enjoyed it. The little children were eager for me to do arts and crafts with them. We built lovely dioramas of the Holy Land. On Mrs. Blaikie's suggestion and expense I also went to East Grinstead to learn shorthand, so that I would have an office skill for America.

Muriel took me to concerts in London where we were guests of her cousin, Anne Blaikie, who was assistant to the Bishop of Gibraltar. The Blaikies' aim was to make a lady out of me.

Then, at long last, my mother and father arrived in London. I went to greet them at the boat train from the Channel. Unlike the time when we parted in Vienna, at this reunion we all cried, tears of joy and relief. We had only one wonderful day together but our joy was beyond description. When we parted they went to Balsham and I returned to the Blaikie house. We were so happy that we all were safely in England.

Papa had a good knowledge of English, and Mutti promised to study hard. Rector Williams was very kind to them. Although they were servants, Rector Williams insisted that they take dinner with the family in the dining room and not with the other servants in the kitchen. The other servants resented that, which made matters difficult for my parents. Mutti, in particular, was miserable.

After two months, Auntie Marjory found them a different job in Horley, very near Copthorne, in the home of a Colonel and his family. The situation there was not much better than at Balsham, but at least they were closer to me. I could go and see them once a week on their day off. From her pitiful pay, Mutti was required to give half her salary to her employers for my father's room and board. He had to work without pay because he did not have a work-permit. English people at the time were not the most sympathetic employers of domestics.

The class system was very much in evidence, and servants were not at all treated as equals. Mutti was appalled by their rude behavior. Once, while walking down the main staircase, she was humiliated by the lady of the house. "Get away, get away!" she screamed. "Don't you know it is bad luck for servants to use the main staircase?" Poor Mutti dissolved in tears. She had employed numerous servants in her lifetime and had never treated them like that. She was a true lady.

Papa was soon very fluent in English. He loved to speak it and to read P.G. Wodehouse in order to learn to be like Jeeves, the model butler. Mutti hardly ever spoke, except to me, when I came to visit, and, of course, to Papa.

The war broke out September third, 1939, with Hitler's Wehrmacht bombing Warsaw. I clearly remember the beautiful sunny day when I saw and heard British planes overhead from Gatwick Airport while riding my bike. I was carrying a red gas mask case over my shoulder, on my way to visit Mutti and Papa. It pained me that Grandma Therese, Aunt Camilla and all my other relatives now were trapped in Nazi Austria, the enemy country. I was so relieved that my parents were now safe and sound in England near me.

Children soon were evacuated from London. People who lived in the countryside were required to take children from London or other big cities into their homes. The Blaikie family accepted more than their share, taking in seven children ranging in ages from six to eleven. I was appointed to take care of the six-year-old twin boys and a seven-year-old girl. My experience at the Day Nursery helped me to handle children and I loved it. These seven children came from slum areas in London, where they spoke with such a pronounced Cockney accent that I could hardly understand them. By the time I left England, however, they spoke the King's English and had learned manners and behaved well. Muriel adored having them; it gave her life purpose.

In October 1939, I received notice that my transit visa was cancelled. I was ordered to leave England. But to where? Mrs. Blaikie helped me write letters to the Immigration Authorities and the Police Departments. I had to appear at the County Seat in Lewis, with all my papers, show them my affidavits from America, and prove to them that the arrival of my visa was imminent.

I received a one-month extension. I wrote to the American Embassy in London telling them about my dilemma. In November my U.S. visa finally arrived. In the meantime, I had applied to the French shipping line for my first-class ticket on the *SS Normandy* and received word back that no passage was available. The French said that the ship was sitting out of service in New York Harbor following an accident. Furthermore they claimed they never had received the money that my parents had paid them. Devastated, I wrote to Miss Fellner at the Children's Refugee Committee, explaining my plight. Her return letter calmed me down. She said she would get their in-house attorney to represent me without charge. In only a week I received a substitute, second-class ticket on the *SS De Grasse*, the smallest ship of the French line. I was thrilled nevertheless.

Mutti, on the other hand, was terrified for me. The Atlantic Ocean was heavily mined by the Germans and their U-boat warfare was deadly. Hundreds of ships were sunk. Transatlantic traffic was risky and extremely dangerous. I told Mutti and Papa that with my visa situation the way it was, I really had no choice. Furthermore, I would gladly take the chance to get to America and start a new life. I promised to find a way to help them come and join me. We could then finally be a family again.

Atlantic Passage and New York City

My departure date was set for November twelfth 1939 at Southampton Harbor. Muriel took me to Southampton the night before. The fog was thick the evening we arrived, and the taxi, driving without lights, had to carefully pick its way through the streets. It was too late for dinner at the hotel, so we went to a fish and chips place. I had never tasted that favorite English fare before, and I enjoyed it. The fried fish and fried potatoes were wrapped in a bag shaped like a trumpet and made from newspaper. We stumbled back to the hotel in the dense fog and talked through the night. Because the boat train would permit only ticketed passengers, Muriel had to stay behind. We were so sad and upset about parting, neither of us noticed that she was still holding my coat when the train pulled out.

Arriving at the dock, I could hardly see the hull of the huge gray ship on the dark, dark sea. A tender transported a few passengers at a time. Our luggage was put into nets and hauled up to the high deck of the vessel. We climbed a rope ladder up the side of the ship to the deck way above. The wind was so strong that the ladders swayed. It was truly scary as I envisioned falling into the black cold water below. Big guns had been installed on the deck; everything was painted gray; and there were sandbags everywhere.

A crewmember took me to my cabin, which was very large, had three beds and nice décor. The purser came and asked if I would like to sell Armistice day poppies to passengers before dinner. What a delightful opportunity to meet other people on board. Of course I jumped at the opportunity. But the purser then asked if I were English, and I had to reply that, in fact, I was now a stateless person, possessing only a certificate of identity from England. I said I really would like to sell the poppies, though. "Mademoiselle, I am sorry, but we need an English lady for that," he said, and with that he left. At dinner I learned that a very tall English girl had been given the fun job.

The seas were extremely rough, and only a few people came to meals—most of the other passengers were too seasick to leave their cabins. The piano in the main lounge slid across the entire room. Dishes crashed to the floor. Ropes were stretched along the decks for passengers to hold on to. The ship creaked and I thought at any minute it would break in half.

The storm never let up. One day we were told to remain in our cabins and we heard guns being fired. I had snuck out and stood at the stern and saw what I thought were torpedoes coming toward us. But they missed us. Later we were told that what we had seen simply was target practice. Of course we knew that wasn't true. The newspapers had been filled with stories about German mines being swept loose in the Atlantic and German U-boats out in droves.

The poppy girl and I became friends and we ate together. We usually were the only people eating in the various restaurants. The large indoor swimming pool was empty of course. There was no entertainment. Most second-class passengers were French and English. Once I went down to third class, where there were many young people from various European countries. They looked as if they were having a lot of fun.

On November twenty-first, we sailed into New York Harbor with all our sirens blowing and everyone on deck. Tenders brought people from shore to come on board. Many of them were newspaper reporters. Quentin Reynolds talked to me. He asked me to put my scarf around my head like a babushka when he took my picture. Looking truly like a refugee, my picture appeared in the Chicago newspapers, with a story that our ship, the *De Grasse*, had been fortunate to evade several U-boat attacks. So much for that story about target practice!

It was close to noon when we were permitted to disembark. This time we walked down the ramp and a huge crowd awaited the people from our ship. When the last person was kissed, hugged and left, I was still there, all alone with my seven suitcases.

I had sent a cable to the Harmel family of New York advising them of my arrival, but I suppose it was censored or it did not arrive. Everyone had left the pier; it was growing dark, I had no American money. I was incapable of carrying all seven suitcases and afraid to leave them. Finally a man walked by and I told him my dilemma. He kindly gave me a nickel for the telephone. I found the number for the Harmels in Brooklyn, and approximately one hour later, Lou Harmel and his handsome son, Merel, came to get me. It was seven o'clock in the evening.

The Harmels had one of those large American cars. As we crossed the Brooklyn Bridge, their car radio was playing Beethoven's Ninth Symphony conducted by Arturo Toscanini. As I watched the lights of the New York skyline, in the company of these two new adoptive relatives and with the familiar music playing, I thought that I had truly arrived in the land where the streets were paved with gold. My new Aunt Hermine welcomed me, commenting that her other son Dick was still at college in Ann Arbor but sent his love.

She also said that Ben Schneider of Chicago would be arriving in New York on business in one week's time and would take me back with him.

Those days in New York passed all too quickly. Lou, Hermine and Merel took me shopping, to the theater and the movies, and showed me New York City. One of Merel's friends invited me to the opera. It could not have been nicer and more exciting. I found myself wishing that I had chosen to stay in New York.

After Uncle Ben completed his business in New York, we boarded a train with sleeping compartments for the seventeen-hour trip to Chicago, where Aunt Kate and Maxine were waiting for us.

Chicago

It was a strange sensation, but, somehow, I sensed that my new family members were disappointed in me. Perhaps I was too tall, too healthy looking, too well dressed, too self-assured to be the poor little refugee girl that they had expected. In comparison, all three of them were very short and Maxine was frail and coughing a lot.

Their twelve-room apartment on Lake Shore Drive was very elegant. There were two maids employed in that household. Maxine's bedroom was huge and gorgeous. I was shown to a tiny room off the kitchen. The window would not open and it looked out into a type of light shaft rather than over Lake Michigan like all the other rooms. I was not used to central heating and I felt too hot and most uncomfortable.

Before I left Vienna, we had gone to the finest leather store, Lederer, to purchase expensive, matching, leather-covered umbrellas, handbags and wallets for Maxine and Kate. I had carried those gifts throughout my eighteen moves. Finally I was able to present it to them, but to my disappointment I never saw them use any of these presents.

They were nice to me, but demonstrated neither the warmth nor the love of the Roseveares or the Blaikies in England. When Maxine went out on dates, she would meet her young men in the lobby downstairs rather than having them come to the apartment where I might meet them.

The morning after my arrival, Aunt Kate awakened me early and we went downtown where, before I knew it, I was put to work as a filing clerk for a chain of ladies clothing stores. I sorted sales checks by state and city so that the proper sales tax could be assigned to them. As a newcomer to the United States, I had to learn that "Soo Cty Ia" really was "Sioux City, Iowa." I just hope that no-one ever got into trouble because of my lack of knowledge.

At noon, the other girls went out to lunch, but I had no money. The five dollars I was allowed to bring with me from England I spent in New York to present the Harmel family with roses. I was too ashamed to ask anybody for money, and at closing time, I found myself in a predicament. I didn't know how to get to the Schneider's apartment. I didn't have a winter coat, and I didn't have carfare. At least I knew the address, and after asking directions, I walked forty long city blocks, approximately five miles in the extreme cold of below freezing weather. I was shivering and my teeth chattered Never had I experienced such a low temperature. The Schneider's asked me why I was so late, they said it was fifteen degrees below zero. I told them what happened, and I coupled it with a request for an advance on my first paycheck. They agreed.

Back in England, the kindly Blaikie family still was thinking of me, I was to learn. I received a lovely note from a woman named Esther Witkowsky, who said she had been advised of my presence in Chicago by a friend in Philadelphia, who had once met and had corresponded with the Blaikies. Not realizing how far Philadelphia was from Chicago, they had asked the friend to look after me. The friend then asked Miss Witkowsky to please accept the responsibility on her behalf. She invited me to visit her, which I was very pleased to do. She turned out to be quite elderly, blind, and one of the most inspiring women it has ever been my privilege to know. Daughter of parents who had immigrated from Germany in the mid-nineteenth century to a lovely old house and garden on a small road that later became Chicago's State Street. She had been among the first three students to enter the University of Chicago. Her mother was an early president of the National Council of Jewish Women and like her, Esther, had a lifelong interest in secular and Jewish affairs. I would take a bus and a train to visit her, spending pleasant Sunday afternoons reading the newspaper to her and discussing world events.

I got a new and better job with a dress manufacturer after Christmas. It paid the same twelve dollars per week, but there I was the model, bookkeeper, phone operator, sales person, stenographer, shipping clerk and all around-girl. Although the sixty-hour-week was extremely long, I enjoyed my employment.

Meanwhile, my parents were still in England and I wanted nothing more than to bring them to safety in the United States, especially knowing how uncomfortable they were with the Colonel and family in Horley, England. Of course, I asked my boss, Sam, to help me but he was in no position to help, owing to the fact that his financial situation was so bad that he sometimes had to ask me to lend him what little money I had saved up. He said, though he couldn't help me, with the necessary papers disclosing his income, perhaps a friend of his by name of Charles Rubin could be of assistance. He set up a lunch date for me to meet Charles, who, as a sales representative, called upon our firm. He was a thirty-three-year-old bachelor, to my mind "an older man."

In the restaurant, I told Charles all about my parents, who in the meantime had been sent to internment camps located on the Isle of Man because, as German citizens, they were considered enemy aliens. Ironically, they were treated exactly like non-Jewish Germans who were Nazis or Nazi sympathizers. Charles listened carefully and volunteered, "I'll be glad to do anything I can to help you." Together we went to the offices of the Hebrew Immigrant Aid Society to fill out papers for affidavits.

The HIAS social worker asked Charles all about his income and family situation. He said that he earned forty-five dollars per week, plus commissions, and had savings of eight-hundred dollars and owned a Chevrolet. The social worker responded that unfortunately his earnings were insufficient to be able to guarantee the welfare of an elderly couple—Papa at the time was fifty and Mutti was forty-eight years old. However, she said, "if you were married, the State Department would consider this to be a reunification of a family unit and your parents would be permitted to enter the United States."

I turned to Charles and asked him: "Would you marry me?" and whispered in his ear that it would only be a formality. Charles looked into my eyes and without a moment's hesitation responded,

"Of course, I'll marry you. All my life I have been looking for a girl like you." This, after our having met only two hours before.

He told the HIAS worker that we were engaged to be married and that we would bring a marriage certificate as soon as we could. They could then start filling out all the necessary documents for my mother's and father's immigration.

Charles invited me to dinner that evening and offered to drive me to my night school class in which Aunt Kate had enrolled me. I went there four nights a week and it became a regular routine for Charles to drive me—who by that time had me calling him Charley. By June 1940, when the Schneiders went to their summer home in Michigan, I had to find a place to stay and rented a room from a Jewish lady with two daughters, while continuing to think of the Schneiders as my family.

Meanwhile, Paul Harmel from Cleveland telephoned to inquire how I was getting along and invited me to come to Cleveland to visit him and his ailing mother. I accepted his offer, hoping to enlist him in my efforts to get affidavits for my parents. I was smitten by this cousin right away. He was a bit shorter than I, but nice looking, very warm and friendly, Harvard-educated, and smart. He was an attorney, had the same name as my girlhood idol in Vienna, Paul, which endeared him to me even more. On Saturday, he took me to a lovely country home owned by friends who welcomed us cordially. We hiked in the woods, and later had a lovely dinner by their huge fireplace.

Paul Harmel told me of friends in Canada who would be willing to provide affidavits for my parents. That meant they would have to go there first, but it might be better than having them wait longer in England. When I took the train home the next day, Paul kissed me good-bye. He then telephoned me at least once a week and occasionally sent me little gifts, a bottle of Shalimar, some gorgeous hankies, candies, and flowers. Aunt Kate thought it was terrible that a man exactly twice my seventeen years would toy with my affections.

He said he wanted to visit me, but that he was prevented to do so because his mother was getting worse and that it would be unwise to leave her. The more we corresponded, the more affectionate his letters became. I told him that Charley wanted to marry me and that I could get my parents over faster that way. I expected him to say that I should not do that, that he would marry me instead. Alas, his answer was that I should follow my heart and do what I thought was right for me.

I did not hide my feelings for Paul from Charley. He responded that he was convinced that I would learn to love him in time, and that in the meantime he had enough love for us both.

On January twenty, 1941, a bitter cold evening, Charley said to me: "Why don't we keep on driving in my new car? It needs a run to keep the motor operating well. We can drive to Hannibal, Missouri, the hometown of Mark Twain, who is one of my heroes. There we can get married without any waiting period. It is a romantic place by the Mississippi River. Would that appeal to you?"

"Yes," I replied

Mr. and Mrs. Charles Rubin

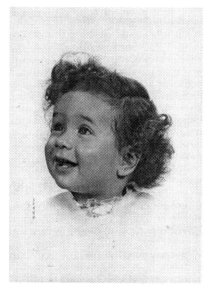

Diana Rubin

Diana's Wedding

Mr. and Mrs. Everett Daly

Mrs. Charles Rubin & Family

New cars had governors on their motors and could not go faster than thirty-nine miles per hour for the first few days. Nevertheless, it was a harrowing ride. The roads were icy and slippery, with many cars and trucks in the ditch on the side of the road. We had to go slowly and Hannibal was far. With a few stops for food or hot coffee, we did not arrive until the next afternoon. When at last we found a justice of the peace, he told us we needed a marriage license from the county seat in New London, miles away, and that they closed at five that afternoon. We got there just minutes before closing time.

I had a great dilemma at the license bureau. The clerk asked for my age and I quickly said eighteen, although I was still six months shy of that. Charley was aghast. He turned to me and said: "I thought you were twenty-three years old! That's what Sam told me. How can I rob the cradle with a teenager?"

"What difference does it make how old I am? You promised to marry me at the HIAS office and now we'll go through with it. I thought you are a man of your word." I spoke firmly, and hoped he was only joking.

The clerk handed us the license and Charley was silent as we drove back to Hannibal. Finally, he said: "Before we go to the J.P., let us stop at the dime store and buy a ring. When we get back to Chicago, my friend Jack, who has a jewelry store, will get me a real diamond ring for you."

At the ring counter at Woolworth's the sterling silver rings cost twenty-five cents. The sales lady asked me whether I wanted a plain one or one with *diamonds*. I chose the plain one.

Then, in a dingy office with a light bulb hanging on a wire from the ceiling, the Justice of the Peace, who was a funny little man, and his wife, who was dressed in a bathrobe, married us.

Charley kissed and embraced me, and it was sweet and comforting. We rented a room at the Mark Twain Hotel, had dinner in their dining room, and then took a walk in the freezing cold, along the icy Mississippi River.

I was totally inexperienced about sex and had never even seen a man in the nude. My husband was sweet, patient and understanding.

In addition to adjusting to each other, Charley's and my first priority as a married couple was to get my parents out of England, where matters had gotten much worse for them. It grated on me, and made me fear for their safety, that Mutti and Papa now were imprisoned on opposite sides of the Isle of Man. They were interned with the same kind of people from whom their escape to England had been necessary in the first place. Imagine, Jews and Nazis were assigned to the same barracks, while the British threw rocks over the barbed wire at them! Papa was told that he possibly could be sent to a camp in Australia, from which he might apply to be sent to Canada. That would be closer to me. He wrote me that he intended to sign up for that opportunity. I responded urging him to please reconsider. In Chicago I was working on trying to get both him and my mother to join us. If he went to Australia, I might never be able to achieve a reunion! And furthermore, after my own experience, I did not want him to have to make two wartime voyages. They simply were too dangerous.

Then, to my horror, I read a story in the *Chicago Tribune* that on an English prison ship en route to Australia some British sailors robbed and beat the German Jews aboard so brutally that some even died. I was so scared that Papa might be on that ship! Luckily, however, he was not. In fact, after reading an account of the same incident, he decided not to go to Australia.

Nothing in my mother's letters from the other side of the island indicated she knew about the unfortunate voyage, and I thought it best not to say anything to her about it.

Although they had learned where the other was within a few days after their interment, my parents were able to speak to and see each other only once in eleven months. Under strict guard, the British escorted the women from the Port Erin facility to the Ramsay internment camp where they were permitted to spend a few hours together.

Conditions in the camps were awful. Particularly where my father was. Because the British did not separate the Jews from the Nazis, my father signed up for the Kosher division where he was not in danger from the Nazis within the barrack. They lived on burned porridge and green apples. They slept on sacks of straw, and had only one thin blanket even though it was very cold on this little island in the middle of the Irish Sea. Nevertheless, there were two benefits for my father. All his life he had suffered from asthma, but on that restricted diet he lost it. He also lost a lot of weight.

My parents, in essence, communicated with each other only through me. Their correspondence to me, called V-mail, could only be eleven lines long per letter and was highly censored. Sometimes there were only eight lines left.

Around this time, (late 1941) my nightmares that lasted the first ten years of my marriage got worse. On occasions I would wake up screaming, after dreaming about Hitler. In some dreams I was in a ditch with corpses; in others, I was running away from him. In one, I actually confronted him with a gun in my hand, unable to decide whether I could really kill anyone, even Hitler. Of course Charley woke up and comforted me until I got back to sleep.

Papa told me that he had learned a lot about human behavior, courage and cowardice from the other men in his barrack. After nine months, he was released from the camp and went to Wales to be near the Roseveare family, who had moved there in the interim. They helped him find cheap living quarters, and I, in what seemed a one-hundred and eighty degree reversal of fortune, sent food packages to him, the Roseveares, the Blaikies and to my cousin Lilian and her husband Lothar.

Mutti spent eleven months in her internment camp, and then was transferred from the camp to a jail in London, which, while she was in it, was all but destroyed during a German air raid. She had to be dug out of the rubble of the jail, and subsequently was permitted to join Papa in Wales. After that, they moved to Manchester where Mutti found a job. Again my father had to work without pay.

The Japanese sneak attack on Pearl Harbor in 1941 brought the United States into World War II. I must confess to having had ambivalent feelings about this. On the one hand, like everyone else in the United States, I was angry and shocked by the Japanese aggression and the loss of innocent American lives in Hawaii. On the other hand, with Hitler still on the loose, I was glad that the weight of the United States would be brought to bear on this conflict, and perhaps end the Nazi reign once and for all.

Charley, meanwhile, was doing well in his job, and I was renewing my love of art as a student at the Art Institute of Chicago. In 1942, I became pregnant, and Charley received notification that he had been classified 1-A and could be called up to military service at any time.

Prior to his date for reporting to the Army, Charley was able to enlist in the Coast Guard, and was assigned to duty on the Great Lakes. I also enlisted in the cause of American patriotism, proudly becoming a U.S. citizen after my twenty-first birthday in 1942.

I swore to myself that I would be a useful member of the citizenry of the most humane and important country in the world. The judge who administered my oath told me: "a pretty girl like you should not have a German name like Hilda, why don't you change it now? It's the only time you can do that without cost. Give yourself an American name like Helen or something like it." Perhaps I should have listened to him.

I sent a letter to the State Department in Washington D.C. to plead for permission for my parents to come to Chicago before my baby was due. The State Department responded in December 1942 that there would be a hearing the following week in Washington D.C. on the subject of my parents' immigration. I was too advanced in my pregnancy to go to Washington.

Charley volunteered to go in my stead but was worried about the outcome of the hearing. He did not want to be blamed if he were not successful. I had full faith in his ability to persuade the officials of the urgency of our family situation—what with me so close to delivering our baby and he so soon to depart for the Coast Guard. He telephoned me from Washington to say that he thought the hearing had gone well, but that we wouldn't know the result until they notified us by mail. Another anxious wait.

Our sweet, tiny baby girl, Diana Ray Rubin, was born January eight, 1943. I had remembered how, when I was a child in Vienna, I admired a statue of the Roman goddess Diana with two deer at her side. It was a beautiful piece of art, and I loved the name of this goddess. So when our beautiful daughter came, we named her Diana

Ray. Ray as a ray of sunshine, and for my grandmothers, Resi and Rosa.

About the same time, we received a favorable reply from the State Department. There was great joy in our household at the prospect of our newly enlarged family being united with my parents. The last diplomatic obstacle had been hurdled. All that separated us from reunification was their booking passage to the United States.

Given the war that was going on, that was far more difficult than it had been for me. After a wait of another nine months, they were finally able to embark on a small Indian vessel that was part of a convoy of twenty-one ships. It was September 1943. The convoy proceeded in three concentric rings. Their ship was in the innermost circle. Around them were mid-sized ships that traveled empty from Europe to the United States, but which brought back supplies on the return leg of the voyage. The outermost circle consisted of destroyers, charged with protecting the convoy. Such voyages typically lasted three or more weeks because instead of following direct courses, the convoys zigzagged to avoid mines and German U-boats and traveled at the speed of the slowest vessels.

We received a telegram that my parents were leaving soon, and we knew that meant that they were leaving the same day. Then we heard a speech by British Prime Minister Winston Churchill that stopped my heart: "As I am speaking now a convoy is being attacked in the Atlantic," he said. I knew right away it had to be the same convoy my parents were on. I cried my eyes out. Inconsolable, I blamed myself for having put pressure on them to take the chance and sail across the Atlantic at a time of such great danger. If only Papa had decided to go to Australia!

Two weeks later, we received a phone call.

Papa and Mutti were on the phone! Laughing and crying, they told me they had just arrived in New York and they would take a train to Chicago, the very next day. Twelve ships in their convoy had been sunk! But the small Indian ship, in the middle of the convoy, had made it safely. A miracle!

It had been four years since I had last seen them in England. Now I had my little family to greet them. Charley and baby Diana and I embraced them at Chicago's Union Station and we were united at last, safe and so very happy.

There was a little furnished apartment waiting for them right across the street from ours. Mutti would not release Diana from her arms. The baby just smiled and showed off her first tooth. At long last, we were all together.

Charley and my parents got along famously. Papa said on more than one occasion that he could not love a biological son more than Charley. My father made many friends, and were it not for the return of his asthma, the situation might have been perfection itself.

As my nanny used to take me to the parks in Vienna, so too, did I develop the habit of going with Diana on daily trips to the park in Chicago. One day, a dog that looked to be a very large fox terrier began to follow us. He was very friendly. I looked on his collar for a dog tag, but he had none. I asked a number of people on the path if they knew to whom the dog belonged, but nobody seemed to know. He was just a stray. Diana and I shared some of our picnic lunch with the dog and gave him some water. The poor dog was ravenous and thirsty.

As I wheeled Diana in her stroller-buggy, the dog followed us all the way to our home. I telephoned Charley at his office and suggested that he call Animal Control to pick up the dog. But by then Diana and I really were enjoying having the dog with us. We decided to keep him and named him Skipper. He was housebroken and a fine companion.

One day Skipper started to play with a cloth dachshund, a toy I had brought with me from Europe. It was a prize that I had won on a cruise ship in Italy in 1937, the year before the *Anschluss,* the little dog was my talisman. Skipper started to shake it and shake it and tore an ear off. He then bit into the dog's body, and *clang, clang, clang,* dozens of gold rings fell from the toy dog as Skipper shook it.

When Mutti came home, she solved the mystery. She told me that she had forgotten that she had stuffed hundreds of gold rings into the toy and shoulder pads and hems of my dresses and coats before I left for England. She had never told me about it. How fortunate I was that the customs people in Austria did not find them. That would have cost me my life! It is understandable, however, that under the extreme stress of the time, people did whatever they thought would help them after their escape. Mutti wanted to help her only child and thought she was protecting me by not telling me about it then. With all the subsequent stress, she forgot about it until the incident with Skipper. To think, I had thought that I had arrived in England with only five dollars in Austrian Schillings and no jewelry!

When the clothes, with gold in the shoulder pads or hems were either worn out or went out of style, I gave them away. Unfortunately, I sold the rings from the toy dog when gold was only thirty-five dollars an ounce.

When the war ended, we were jubilant. Like so many European families, we tried to learn what we could about the fate of our relatives, particularly my sweet little grandmother, Therese Kohn and my mother's sister, Camilla Gruenwald, my favorite aunt. We wrote to their old address but the letters came back "addressee unknown." We contacted many different organizations, to no avail. By now we feared the worst—that they all had perished in concentration camps.

Return to Vienna

I begged Charley to take me back to Vienna, to look for my family members that had not been heard from since 1939. Everyone advised us against going back too soon. It might be too dangerous or too difficult. The State Department added to our concern. In a letter, it informed me that if I went, it would be at my own risk. Reminding me that the city had been divided into four post-war zones by the Americans, British, French and Russians, the letter cautioned that if I were apprehended in the Russian sector of Vienna, the State Department could not protect me. As I was born in Vienna, Russia would not acknowledge my American citizenship. It was the height of the Cold War but, nevertheless, in 1949, we actually were on our way to Austria, a trip that would include stops in Switzerland, Italy and England.

Our travel agent in Chicago had not been able to get us a hotel reservation in Vienna, but I was not worried. After all it was my city and I knew my way around. Surely I could get us a room in a nice hotel. Our flight arrived late in the evening.and it was raining hard. The airport seemed very primitive to me, having become used to our large airports in Chicago and New York The hotel information counter was closed. So, we took a taxi into the heart of the city by the Opera. I knew I could get a hotel there easily, but I realized I did not know which zone was which.

We had the taxi take us from one big hotel to the other, no luck. Everything was filled up. There were some big meetings going on, the driver told us. He said he knew a nice small hotel by the fountain of the Magic Flute in the fourth district, my old home district. They had a room for us and it was lovely. The room clerk asked for our passports and said they had to go to the Police Station, as we were in the Russian Zone. What a dilemma! I quickly asked for my Passport back and said I'd go to the Police Station with the clerk. He agreed and off we went into the rain. Our taxi had left. After waiting a while, we got another one and got into the Police Station. There the policeman asked why I had come with the clerk and I said I needed to be with my passport at all times. He laughed and stamped it. We went back to the hotel.

We had been on our way for many, many hours and the excitement and also the worry contributed to complete exhaustion. We slept until noon the next day. We were only ten minutes walk from my old apartment house and of course I wanted Charley to see it. So did I. The opera building had been set on fire when the Germans retreated from Vienna and the Russians came into the city from the east. Now it was being rebuilt to look exactly as before, but overall, the city was gloomy.

My old apartment building was standing but neighboring buildings were in ruins. It had been eleven years since I left. I loved being back there and hated it all at the same time. My father's antique store was now a bicycle store. I rang the bell to our old apartment, but there was no reply. Some former neighbors came down the stairs as we were ascending to the floor above. "Hilda!" they said and put their arms around me. The way our neighbors had treated us after the *Anschluss* came back to me. I felt revolted. and did not know how to be released fast enough.

"Hilda, did you see what happened to our beautiful city? The Americans did that to us. Isn't it terrible what they did?"

Charley looked at me and I stared back at him. Did I hear them correctly? They did not say how are you, where have you been, where are your parents, your grandparents? How did you survive? They wanted me to pity them. How ludicrous!

I was searching for an answer and all I could muster was: "It was terrible what you did to us" and we left.

Charley took my hand and we walked through what used to be our lovely garden and now was a gray ugly space with huge garbage cans. The caryatids holding up our landlord's balcony were gone and the walls had huge patches of deterioration.

It was a sad scene but I felt it was the right kind of scene. It was still less than they deserved.

The mother-in-law of my cousin Fritz in Haifa, in the new nation of Israel, lived a block away and we were to have lunch with her. Frau Dora Halpern and her husband had returned to Vienna from Haifa, and managed to get their apartment building back. Charley and I walked over and climbed the four flights and Mezzanin, making it five flights, and were received warmly by "Tante Dora," the name she asked us to call her.

She did not speak English, so I interpreted for Charley. Dora was a lively charming lady and we enjoyed her company immensely. Her husband was a patient in the hospital so we paid him a visit there.

The entire fourth district was in the Russian Zone but Dora did not seem to think it was a problem for her. We saw some Russian soldiers, who were huge Mongolian types with fur hats, large guns, bullet belts across their shoulder, and to my eyes, very intimidating looking characters. But during the next five days we had no problem going from zone to zone without noticing any kind of demarcation.

We ate in the Rathauskeller, the famous restaurant in the City Hall. Charley loved the real Wiener Schnitzel and Krautsalat. In Vienna, lunch was the main meal of the day. I had recovered from my emotional encounter with my former neighbors, thanks to Dora's pleasant conversation.

The following morning we went to the main police station to find out what happened to my family. Sure enough they had records; they were good at keeping records. My grandmother, my Aunt Camilla, her husband, several of my cousins and other aunts on my father's side of the family, all had been deported to Lublin, Poland, and the terrible concentration camps there, where no one survived.

It was no surprise to us. However, hearing it officially was still a horrible shock. Every person in Vienna was now my enemy all over again. Did I ever live there really; did I ever love it there? Did I ever think of these people as my friends? Everything was so familiar and so alien at the same time.

People seemed to be speaking a foreign language. Not the German I was used to, but much more the Viennese dialect that only uneducated people used when I was young. I could hardly understand them. Or did I not wish to understand them?

Before I had left Vienna, we were ordered to eliminate foreign words from our speech. Because the crowned heads of Europe had used French as the language at court, French words interspersed in your sentences were considered elegant and used by educated people. It was then frowned upon and considered traitorous. Viennese ladies of means went shopping in Paris for hats and dresses. But Hitler wanted people to wear their national dress. That meant Dirndls and Lederhosen. Gone was the *chic* of Viennese women. With Jewish artists, actors, Musicians, designers, and there were many, gone from Vienna, Viennese cultural events had lost their spark. Vienna, now arianized, had changed a lot, and not for the better.

I did not voice my feelings to Charley. He knew me well enough to see that I was having a difficult time and I didn't want to spoil his trip. We visited the museums, the palaces, the parks, the Vienna Woods. We went to two operas, two concerts and an operetta. Vienna was on its way back to recovery from the war. I was not at all certain that I would ever be.

About a year later, we learned that Mutti's brother, Rudi, had survived. Mutti was doing alterations in a store owned by German Jewish refugees in Chicago. When a customer named Mautner came in, Mutti commented that a Mautner family had lived in a town neighboring Lassee, where she grew up. He responded that he was from that family, and that he had just come from Montevideo, Uruguay, where he had lived since 1938.

More conversation about their families produced the information that her brother Rudi was alive and living with his wife and daughter in Montevideo. Furthermore, Mr. Mautner said, Rudi and his family had converted to Catholicism and did not mingle with the Jews of Montevideo. However, he said he could get her Rudi's address, which he did.

Mutti came home all excited and Papa said: "Rudi is a no-good guy! Try to remember how he did not want to give you your rightful inheritance and how you had to go to court to get it! And why didn't he ever contact you or your mother and sister in Vienna? Forget about him, like he forgot about you and us!"

I was upset by what Papa had said and shouted: "We must let bygones be bygones. It has been so many years. We must write to him!" Mutti agreed with me, saying: "After all he is my brother!"

We wrote to them. They had changed their name from Kohn to Kuehne and told us that Ilse, their daughter, who was then about sixteen, had fallen in love with a young handsome American Mormon missionary who had persuaded them to become members of the Church of Latter Day Saints. They asked us to help them come to Chicago.

I was pregnant and not feeling well at all. I subsequently lost the baby in my seventh month, but I ran around in Chicago's one hundred degree heat and got affidavits for them. They arrived in winter. We had a big celebration, and paid a month's rent for a small apartment right across the street from us. We gave them what winter clothes we could spare. My new Mouton Lamb coat looked great on my young cousin Ilse and I gave it to her.

We asked many questions. Why had he converted to Catholicism? Why had they never contacted us in Vienna? Rudi responded that when he had to turn his farm over to the Nazis in Lassee, similar to the way my father was forced to sign over our antique store, the local priest told him that he would help his family get to Montevideo if they would convert. As for never contacting us, he told me that his wife Lizzi's mother, Frau Gottlieb from Lassee, and her crippled son Richard, were also stuck in Vienna. Since he could not get them out, though he had tried, he gave up on his mother, sister and all of them. I was appalled.

After Charley and I moved to Highland Park, Mutti and Papa also had to relocate to another apartment building in Chicago. Rudi, who had found a good job in Chicago, rented in a different neighborhood.

I shall never forget the time Rudi made an announcement after he and his family had dinner with us. He told us: "we need to break contact with you since you are too Jewish. We don't want this for our daughter. Therefore do not try to be part of our family any more." They all got up and left without a thank you or goodbye. After we recovered from that speech Papa said: "I told you, a leopard never changes his spots." Mutti cried and cried relentlessly.

Living under the Nazis had different effects on different Jews. Some felt even more resolute about being Jewish. Others felt they could win acceptance in the Gentile world by casting off their Jewish identities. Our family connection was severed. I wish it were not so, but I have learned to accept that some things can not be changed.

Adlai Stevenson

One day in 1958 when I returned home from grocery shopping, Mutti was aflutter. "You are never home when important messages are for you," she said, "Adlai Stevenson called, disappointed that he could not speak to you. He said that he had to go out of state, but will call again when he returns."

It was my turn to be flabbergasted. "*Adlai Stevenson? The Adlai Stevenson*? The one whom the Democrats ran twice against President Eisenhower? Mutti, are you sure heard the message right?"

"Of course it was Adlai Stevenson," she responded indignantly. "My hearing is just fine thank you, I could not make up a name like that."

As Mutti and I began unloading the groceries, I thought that perhaps someone who knew how much I admired Stevenson, a former governor of Illinois, had been playing a practical joke on me. Maybe it was Charley. But I couldn't get the thought out of my mind; what if it really was Governor Stevenson? Could he have seen my paintings at the art show in Libertyville, where he lives? Wow! Wouldn't that be something if he wanted one of my paintings?

Cuckoo!, Cuckoo! Cuckoo! For a moment I thought that the clock that Charley and I had purchased for Diana in Switzerland was commenting on my reveries, but no, it simply was announcing the time. It meant that Diana would be coming home from high school soon, and either Mutti or I would drive with her to the Chicago hospital where Papa was being treated for one of his severe asthma attacks. Mutti had been staying with us since Papa had been hospitalized when his asthma got worse, and we took turns visiting him. Charley, Mutti, Papa, Diana and I felt so close to each other, I couldn't imagine anything bad happening again to our family, not after all we had been through during the Nazi years.

Some days later, while Diana was chattering about her day at school, Mutti mentioned the mysterious phone call from Adlai Stevenson. "Mother," said our pragmatic American daughter "why do you agonize whether or not it really was Governor Stevenson? Why not just telephone him and say you are returning his call. If it wasn't he, then he'll tell you so." She retrieved the telephone book and found the listing for Stevenson's law offices in Chicago.

The next day I telephoned, and Newton Minnow, his law partner, took the phone call. Minnow told me he recognized my name because I once had done a watercolor portrait of his daughter at the Winnetka Art Fair.

When we were living in Chicago I attended the School of the Art Institute of Chicago, which I could do because Mutti came home from her nearby workplace to give Diana lunch at noon. When we moved to Highland Park's North Shore I attended numerous art classes in Winnetka and Evanston, taught by well known artists. As a matter of fact I never stopped going to art workshops and classes where ever I found them, even though I was already teaching art. I used to hone my skills by painting watercolor portraits of people for the Red Cross as a volunteer at Great Lakes Naval Hospital. At art fairs in Chicago and suburbs, for two and a half dollars each!

Mr. Minnow said yes, he knew that the former governor Adlai Stevenson had tried to get in touch with me, who was interested in looking at my paintings. Minnow said he would tell the governor I had returned his call as soon as he came back from Poland. We were thrilled.

These were heady times for me, as my reputation as an artist grew. One time I was showing my paintings and lecturing to the Hadassah chapter in Glencoe, Illinois. A listener was particularly taken with a painting in which I portrayed a meeting of the *Sanhedrin*, a great ancient Jewish lawmaking body. She pointed to one of the figures, saying it looked exactly like her father-in-law, who had been a rabbi in Vienna. Indeed, that's who it was, as Rabbi Mandel had been the rabbi in my synagogue. I learned that the woman's husband, Dr. Mandel, who was the new chief of staff at a big hospital in Chicago, was the rabbi's son. Later he became my own father's physician.

When Mrs. Mandel told me her maiden name, I realized that her younger brother had actually gone to a school dance with me at high school. She also told me that Paul my idol of Vienna days had immigrated to Washington D.C., living in fact next to Rabbi Mandel's widow, her mother-in-law. Curious what had transpired in

Paul's life—well, perhaps more than curious—I asked if she could get me Paul's telephone number.

Unfortunately, Papa did not get better. The new asthma medication was too strong for his heart and he died in 1958. We were devastated, poor Mutti especially, they were inseparable and she always had described Papa as her best friend. Papa was only sixty-nine years old. He loved life, especially in his new country with his little family and our dog Bijou.

He had made so many friends and had loved his business. He adored Diana and both Papa and Mutti lavished their love on me, their only child. He was proud of my work and used to tell me: "Some day you will be a famous painter!" And most of all he was proud of his American citizenship. He had said so the last time he had visited us in Highland Park, before being admitted to the hospital. I just could not imagine life without him.

Mutti not only had lost her husband and best friend when Papa died, she also had lost her bridge partner. We persuaded her to move in with us. Mutti taught Diana how to play bridge. We were so happy to have her with us and she loved it, too. Our den was transformed into a cozy room for Mutti. She loved her space, and also took over the kitchen without a word of objection from me. Her cooking not only was better than mine, it gave me more time to paint. Diana happily drove Mutti places; no grandmother was more doting, no granddaughter more loving.

I, too, had every reason to be happy with Charley, who spoiled me and often flattered me with comments about how beautiful he found me to be, how talented, generous, loving, brilliant, a perfect mother, a perfect wife, reliable, honest, and loyal. It made me laugh, but I loved hearing it anyway. I would regularly meet his train from Chicago. He so enjoyed seeing me at the Highland Park station with Bijou. Charley would sprint from the train to us. He never walked, always ran. Bijou would pull at his leash, so eager to greet Charley that I could hardly hold him.

"Hilda, Sweetheart!" he would greet me. "Am I glad to see you! Have you been waiting long? It's so wonderful seeing you standing there when I get off the train. I'm the luckiest guy in the world!" He would kiss me, and pet the dog, and I would give him the car keys as we walked to the parking lot. He would tell me about the progress with his gin rummy game with Walter, a neighbor with whom he would ride to the train station in the morning. In the evenings Walter would go in the opposite direction to meet his wife for dinner at her parents.

Charley and I enjoyed our train station routine, which gave us a little time alone before going home to Mutti and Diana. Sometimes, out of their earshot, we discussed our plans for remodeling our house. Although we were comfortable in the house, after Mutti moved in, we began to wish we had an additional bathroom. Also, I felt that my home studio space was neither large nor bright enough. So we decided to get a builder to do the job. We added a full bath to our bedroom and enlarged the back section of the house. This required us to put some furniture in the garage, while bedroom and living room walls were torn down. At one point, Diana moved temporarily to a friend's house, so we could stay in her room. The house was in a total mess.

And wouldn't you know it, on the worst day of the disarray in our house, Governor Stevenson telephoned—ten months after his original phone call—to say he would like to drop by that very afternoon as he would be having dinner later in Lake Forest, a little to the north of us.

I was so happy to receive his call, but how could I have him come into a disaster area like our home? I was very apologetic and explained the situation to him. He said that if he were to postpone his visit today, he might not be able to reschedule it for a month or more because he once again was leaving for Europe. "Please don't worry about the disarray," he said. "I really do not mind. All I want is to see your paintings and choose one for my living room. I have just the spot over the table with my Lincoln memorabilia on it." Well, of course I could not say no, to this man who I felt should have been the President of the United States!

He anticipated that he would arrive at our house in about four hours. It was a beautiful spring day and our backyard hedge was in full bloom with forsythias. I cut down all the blooming branches and planted them in the rubble of the missing back wall. It looked great!

A number of my neighbors and other residents of Highland Park had purchased some of my paintings. I telephoned them and asked if I could borrow them to show to Governor Stevenson. If he were to choose their painting, I would return two for one. They all agreed to my proposal. Charley picked up their paintings for me, and I moved workmen's ladders from the garage to the living room, to put my paintings on them. It set them off beautifully against the delightful yellow flowering branches.

Several of my friends and neighbors and their children wanted to know if they could come and meet Stevenson, but I was absolutely firm. "Sorry," I said, "This is a business deal, not a campaign stop." They understood. At four-thirty an old Oldsmobile pulled into the driveway and I went out to meet my illustrious guest. So, too did Bijou, who barked. "No Bijou, bad dog!" I was embarrassed. "Please don't worry, I love dogs," the governor said, petting the dog and stretching his hand out to me. He wore a suit with a vest and an old-fashioned watch chain laced through his vest buttonhole. He looked like someone's kind and gentle uncle. Mutti, Diana and Charley were inside where I introduced them all.

He engaged each one of us in conversation, as if we had met before and had all the time in the world. "My what a grand garden you have!" he said at one point.

Diana was thrilled that she had the chance to talk to such a famous gentleman about her having won the Illinois State Latin contest again, this her third time. The governor told her he was impressed by that.

He also took the time to chat with my mother about Vienna and asked Charley about his textile business.

Before inspecting my paintings, he talked with me about the exhibit of Winston Churchill's paintings at the Art Institute of Chicago. Should a prestige institution like that museum give him a show just because of his celebrity and not because of the merit of his paintings?

When he looked at the paintings, he told me he had been thinking about one he had seen at the art show in Libertyville, but now wanted to see them all. He wandered around looking very earnestly at every one of the twenty I had put onto the ladders for display. After what seemed a long time, but probably was no more than ten minutes, he removed three paintings from the ladders. "I cannot decide which one I should choose; they are all so lovely," he said.

"Why don't you take these three home with you and you can call me to pick up the ones you decide against?" I suggested. I would have been delighted for the opportunity to see him again.

He now put one of them aside, thereby narrowing his choice to a landscape of Galena, Illinois, and another that I had named "Woman With Blue Cat." He said he loved them both. I didn't wish to interfere and let him come to his own conclusion. Finally he said, "My father had a little newspaper in Galena. The way you have captured the different levels of the town, connected by endless staircases, is very appealing to me. I have often been to Galena and remember it fondly. Or is that the wrong reason to choose a work of art?"

"There are no wrong reasons for choosing a painting you will live with," I responded. "One is always subjective."

He smiled and asked me not to wrap the picture, because it would be fine in the back seat of his car.

The governor made some very flattering remarks about my paintings, which boosted my confidence in my work. I had admired this man for a long time and had hoped that he would be president of our country. If only Papa could have been there with us!

Several children had been waiting in front of our house and when we emerged, they ran up and asked for autographs. Ricky, the little boy from across the street, had just lost his two front teeth, and now he lisped: "Mr. Stevenson, you have been in there so long, I did not have any supper!" The governor smiled and patted the boy's head. "Now you will eat twice as much when you get home. It was so nice of you to wait for me." Meanwhile, Charley had indeed wrapped the painting protectively and placed it onto the back seat of the Oldsmobile.

Charley, Mutti, Diana and I went to our favorite little restaurant, near the Ravinia station, to celebrate, then came home after supper to clear the decks. It had been a long and exciting day and we were exhausted. The workmen were coming early the next morning and the paintings had to be taken off their ladders.

Although we decided against alerting the *Highland Park News* before Stevenson's visit, we filled in the newspaper on the details afterward, and its write-up, along with other stories that they had been kind enough to write about me, helped spread my reputation locally.

Additionally I taught art classes for adults and children at the YWCA and later on at the Highland Park Art Center.

Teaching helped me to learn by forcing me to formulate my ideas and to share my enthusiasm for art with my students. It also generated more sales of my work. I taught three classes each week to separate groups of twenty-four students. The classes were always filled, causing us to have waiting lists.

How different my childhood interests were from those of my daughter's generation. We, who grew up before television, had to rely on books and radio to make use of our imagination and to conjure up our own mental images in order to illustrate what we heard or read. We were trained image makers, while children in the post-television age, for the most part, were passive receivers of images, rather than senders.

Most art educators believe in the native creativity of all children, not just the artistically gifted. I believe that without creativity, we lose our motivation for living enjoyable lives. Increasingly, adults are going to painting classes, in part to make up for the creative gap left by their childhood education.

I was told that the ancient Chinese artists developed some interesting criteria for excellence in painting. In their hierarchy of judgment, the bottom rung of the artistic ladder was *craftsmanship*. The middle rung was represented by *taste*. The pinnacle, or highest rung, was *vision*. I believe that these ancient Chinese were truly discerning. The more complete the artist is as a person, the better he will be able to communicate through his work. Technical skill alone does not make an artist. A painting, skillfully executed by a craftsman who has nothing to say, still says nothing.

One person whom I always wanted to teach, my daughter Diana, had no interest in art. She had plenty of creativity, but it ran in a different channel. Diana always had a mind for business. In elementary school, a teacher taught a little bit about stocks and bonds to the children. While the other pupils may soon have forgotten about it, Diana found the idea of investing fascinating. She started reading stock reports. With her savings account money, she purchased three shares of Superior Oil.

In high school she was an honor student. She applied to Cornell, Stanford and the University of Pennsylvania, writing in her college essays about her fascination with business and the stock market. Only Penn accepted her, perhaps because of that essay. She would have preferred Stanford, I believe, but the Wharton School also had its attractions. It had an excellent curriculum in finance. Furthermore, she didn't have to enroll in one of Wharton's statistics classes to understand how favorable her odds were. She was one of only three women admitted to her class, compared to hundreds of men.

AL CAPP PRESENTING Hilda Rubin with an award given her by the Immigrants Service League for her contribution to her adopted country. Mrs. Rubin, who lives at 1184 Beech lane, is the subject of a story in the January issue of "American Aritst" Copies of the national publication which traces the artist's background in Vienna to her current studio-home in Highland Park, will be available at the Highland Park Library.

NS Group Photo by Milton Merner

Never envisioning she would meet her former Vienna neighbor, the ex-Austrian Chancellor Dr. Kurt von Schuschnigg at tea in Lake Forest, Mrs. Charles (Hilda) Rubin, Right, Beech Ln,., North Shore artist, finds her recent visit with the international figure fascinating.

Brushes with Celebrities

In 1961, I personally met Kurt von Schuschnigg, the former Chancellor of Austria, at a lecture he gave at Lake Forest College, Illinois. I had a chance to speak with him, and he asked if I had been one of the little girls who had marched in the Nazi parades. No, I told him, I was a little girl who had been forced by the Nazis to scrub the sidewalk clean of swastikas along with my mother. I was a little girl at whom bystanders threw rocks. He did not answer but later I received a couple of letters from him.

November 9, 1961:

Verehrte Gnaedige Frau (Honored Gracious Lady).

I was most thrilled to meet you and only regret that there was not time enough for what we used to call a "Plausch' (chat). It is always a nice experience talking about the accustomed common surroundings of past years. On the other hand it is frightening and oppressive time and again to suspect many tragic moments and losses, which nobody can ever forget and yet everybody tries hard not to think about. It was our curse living in the most inhuman time, and blessing to discover this—sometimes a little strange—but always-most-human country. All good wishes and respectful regards for you and your work.

Handkuesse von Ihrem aufrichtigen (hand kisses from your sincere),

Kurt Schuschnigg

On another day, I received a telephone call while at home in Highland Park. The man on the phone said that he was calling on the suggestion of Anne Blaikie, a cousin of the family that I had stayed with in England for nine months. He was attending a conference in nearby Evanston, Illinois, and, of course, I invited him to visit us. He turned out to be the Bishop of Gibraltar, whose assistant Anne Blaikie, was a cousin of the Blaikie's in Copthorne. We had a wonderful, most interesting evening with the bishop at our home. He was easy to talk to and very charming.

There was a story in *Time* magazine in 1962 about the Bishop of Ghana having called President Kwame Nkrumah "the Anti-Christ" for which he earned temporary expulsion from Ghana. Charley noticed that the prelate was referred to as "Bishop Roseveare." My husband wondered if the bishop might be a relative of my "English family." Intrigued, I decided to write to Bishop Roseveare and ask him. I did not have his address but simply addressed my letter to: the Bishop of Ghana, at Accra.

He actually received the letter, and by return mail he told me that he indeed was a first cousin of my "Uncle" Bill Roseveare in England. He knew about Bill Roseveare, having this little Jewish refugee girl living in his home, me. The Bishop asked me to send him the magazine, and I sent him three copies of *Time*. Also his letter was signed with what I thought was a plus symbol and the name Richard. I took the letter to my Art Class, in which one of my students, an Episcopalian lady read it. She said; that only bishops may sign with a cross and their first name. The symbol was not a plus but a cross. How was I to know? I didn't usually correspond with bishops.

Rob Roseveare, my adoptive "cousin" in whose room I had stayed in England while he was away at school, subsequently visited the Bishop in Ghana. Rob also had an interesting career following his graduation from Cambridge University. He held positions, both in the Ministry that was Britain's equivalent to the U.S. Department of Energy, and also served as a diplomat in Britain's U.S. Embassy with responsibility for international oil affairs.

In 1967, Rob visited us in Highland Park, Illinois—the first time we actually had met face to face. Later that year, he was appointed Secretary of the British Steel Corporation and in time became one of its Managing Directors. In 1977, Queen Elizabeth II conferred upon him the honor of Commander of the Order of the British Empire (CBE). He retired in 1983. Rob's wife, Paddy, was just ten years old when the war broke out. In 1940 she and her sister were evacuated by their father to Canada along with other English children. I have been a guest in their home several times and visited them with Norm and also with Herman. We are in constant touch by mail. I am very proud and honored that they allow me to feel that I am part of their family.

Making a Career in Art

Charley and I married just nine months after I came to America. During those months I worked very hard at my jobs but enjoyed it. I went to night school five times a week. My new husband insisted that I not go to work any more, that he was making enough money to support both of us. He also wanted me to do what I truly loved doing, and that was to attend the school of the Art Institute of Chicago, in the famous Museum. A friend joined me and we enrolled in classes on Saturdays and some evenings

To be a full time student was far too expensive and time consuming for me. I now had a household to maintain. I found the instructors did not teach like the professors had taught in Europe. We mainly had to work from still-life setups or nude models without being given any kind of instructions. We just did what we could, and sometimes the teacher would stop at our easel and make a short comment.

I had never used oil paints before but nobody told us how to mix colors or use the brush or palette knife. I spent most of my time watching what the other students did. But somehow my work did improve. At this time I decided that I wanted to become a dress designer and sketch artist for dress manufacturers. After two years I changed schools. It was my desire to have a profession and not just be a housewife.

I enrolled for a full-time program at the Vogue School of Design, since the Art Institute had given up the dress design department in their class schedule. At Vogue School the classes not only taught drawing elongated models turning around their own axis in typical modeling stances on the runways, but great emphasis was put on making flat patterns of dress designs and of course sewing. We also had to learn to drape fabric on dummies for designs. That part I enjoyed the most. During the two years I spent there I learned a lot, but did not want to be a dressmaker, nor make flat patterns. I only wanted to draw my designs. In the Chicago dress market there was no demand for sketch artists. They were hired mainly in New York. I did however want to complete my course and graduate as a dress designer.

In 1950 we were given notice by our landlord to leave our apartment. The building was sold and the new owner wanted to make it his home. We had made many improvements to our apartment, and my parents lived next to ours, which was a wonderful convenience. Now, all of us had to leave, and there was a severe shortage of rentals. We were forced to buy a house and landed on Beech Lane in Highland Park, our home for the next ten happy years. Since both my parents had jobs they stayed in Chicago, where they found a place to live.

I did not graduate from the Vogue School, but enrolled in various art classes in Winnetka and Evanston, suburbs near Highland Park, where there were many fine, well known artists teaching classes. I loved the atmosphere and comradery in those classes, and became good friends with the artists and other students. I learned far more than I ever had before. My work was being admired and I won a prize here and there and exhibited in outdoor art fairs. As a volunteer for the Red Cross, I also painted watercolor portraits of the wounded soldiers and sailors at Great Lakes Naval Hospital for several years. My oil paintings started to sell well at art fairs. After submitting my work to juried shows I was also accepted at the Art Rental and Sales Gallery at the Art Institute of Chicago, where my paintings were on exhibit and for rental or sale.

Through Girl Scouts, for whom I served as the Arts and Crafts Chairman of Lake County, I met the director of the YWCA in Highland Park and she invited me to come and teach art classes there. Later I also taught at the Highland Park Art Center. In all I spent over twenty years teaching art, while painting up a storm in my studio, participating in exhibits and giving lectures on art and artists. We traveled a lot and visited the major Museums of the world. Though I was a devoted mother, wife and daughter, my passion was my painting.

Oskar Kokoschka

Hilda in Salzburg

Hilda

Hilda and O. K.

Oskar Kokoschka

In the summer of 1962, I went to Salzburg, Austria to study watercolor painting at the International Seminar with Oskar Kokoschka, the world famous German Expressionist artist. I subsequently wrote an article about this remarkable experience for the *Chicago Tribune*'s Sunday Magazine. The cover of the magazine reproduced my painting of Salzburg, while the twelve-page article was illustrated with more of my works.

The article, appearing in the May 5, 1963 edition, was titled:

"One Summer in Salzburg"

By Hilda Rubin

Over the loudspeaker the name came like a thunderclap. "Kokoschka." He was on his way up from the old city of Salzburg, riding the long track of the cable car to the

medieval fortress "Kokoshchka's castle. We, the 280 artists, who had come from all over the world for his summer seminar, called it that.

My father often had told me about his classmate the furious painter who had rocked Vienna at the turn of the century with his wild writings and wilder paintings. By the time I had reached my teens, his work was accepted; he was Austria's gift to the world. In 1938, the year I had escaped to England as a refugee from Hitler, Oskar Kokoschka chose England as his place of voluntary exile.

Now, in summer, I had come back to the land of my birth, to the city of Mozart and the mountains of my childhood, to the fortress that dominated all of us that summer.

I had come from Zurich to Salzburg by train—twelve hours winding through mountains hidden by rain and fog into a gray city of rain. On a strangely cold July evening I walked thru the dark, narrow streets where others huddled close to the ancient buildings. In the Loden coats, or capes, they looked like ghosts on unhappy errands ... like ghosts of other summers in girls' camps near Salzburg when I heard the first rumblings of a Nazi underground whose idol lived just a mountain away in Berchtesgaden.

Somewhere behind the pall of the fog were the mountains, and the fortress on the hill loomed like an ominous monster of black, wet rock.

All that wakeful night, I kept asking: "Why have I left my home to come to this beautiful but dismal city? I had spent half my life in Austria, yet I was a stranger.

The next morning the bells from the church tower outside my window almost made me fly out of bed. I looked across the little square to Mozart's house and up the hill. The fortress was bathed in early sunlight, and the mountains seemed close enough to touch.

The city had come to life. There was a buzzing and ripping of cars and motorcycles. Buses spewed out chattering, camera-laden tourists, and women in colorful dirndls and men in Lederhosen. Seeing them I caught my breath. These peasant costumes had always been characteristic of Salzburg. But in my city, Vienna, they had become a national costume only in the late 30's, the civilian costume approved by the Nazi party. Now—looking from my window at the magnificent city of domes and spires ringed by snowcapped mountains, at the river that raced and flashed through the alpine valley, a river whose graceful bridges shimmered like bracelets on a woman's arm—I felt an old fear.

"It is going to be all right," I said. "I love this town."

But a week later, when July turned warm, the sight of white knee socks still chilled my spine.

And the gnarled, cold hard faces I had seen only in iron curtain countries—were these merely the everyday look of a weather-beaten mountain people—serious, gloomy, withdrawn? Or were they the new faces of old enemies?

At home, my husband, my mother, and I had talked it all out. I would enjoy the mountains and the festivals. I would study with the Italian group—partly to improve my Italian and partly because I had found that Italians are among the warmest, friendliest, most creative people in Europe. I would not mingle with those who reminded me of the past. After all, I was an American. I would simply throw myself into my work.

All seminar students had been enrolled in language groups—English, French, Italian and German—all under the supervision of Kokoschka's assistant instructors. We had one wing of the huge fortress that had been built during three centuries by the ruling prince-archbishops; five floors of studios, cafeteria and offices; spacious rooms with gothic ceilings, whitewashed walls, new lighting, and a public address system. The huge, handcarved doors had locks as big as television screens. The vistas from the ramparts, the ancient chapel, the arches, the walls and towers all made me feel like an actor in some medieval pageant. Visiting the studios was like going from country to country; the language changed from group to group, and so did the people.

We were assigned to our studios and left to work up a backlog of water-color sketches before Kakoschka arrived. Thirty models, ranging in age from fifteen to 65 and each better than the other, changed their poses every fifteen minutes. The changes were clocked by the glockenspiel below, by the smallest bells of the fortress chapel, and by the booms of the cathedral bells down the hill.

I worked hard, and I was happy among the Italians and French. They laughed and joked. Between poses they exchanged ideas about color and form.

But when I discovered that my Italian was no better than the Italian assistant's English, and that I understood little of the technical lectures and announcements on the loudspeaker, I decided I had to move.

The English group was too large—more than 75 people in a poorly lighted studio, elderly ladies or angry young men or youngsters interested mostly in each other.

So I found a small but beautiful room occupied by a German-speaking group. I moved my equipment down five flights of narrow, winding stairs—two stools, my easel, jars of water, paints, a raincoat, a smock, my portfolio and stand, overshoes, paper and 150 sketches. Kokoschka was to arrive the next day and I wanted to be ready.

No one in the new studio bade me welcome. Wherever I put my easel I seemed to be in somebody's way.

We worked in silence for the next few hours. No one spoke except a young blond giant of a boy who kept giving directions to the model. At last I walked over, looked at his work, and found it excellent. I said so, in German-German with an American accent.

His reply astonished me. "We Germans," he said caustically, "can take true criticism. We do not need a pat on the back like Americans, to whom everything is very nice and very interesting..."

For days I had been speaking several languages, all of them with an American accent; in my speech I seemed to belong nowhere. Yet I had a home in America, the love of my family, respect for my work—and then a remark by an arrogant boy opened wounds I thought had healed; the terror of losing home and belongings, of fleeing from country to country, of losing 30 members of my family in gas chambers.

What was I to do?

Forget. My family and I had agreed on that. See Salzburg like a tourist. Avoid the unpleasant. Work. I tried to concentrate on my work, and not on the unimportant, prosaic things such as; that the sanitary conditions were primitive: cold water, no soap, and a roll towel that was changed only once a week. The cafeteria served 900 meals a day, but the dishes were washed in a single bucket of water and the silverware merely wiped.

During lunch I suggested that perhaps we could provide paper towels and soap; weren't we always covered with paint or clay?

We were indeed, I was told. But Europeans do not need to be wrapped in cellophane, like American cheese! By mid-afternoon everyone in the studio had made an aggressively anti-American remark. Hiroshima, Little Rock. Imperialist, warmonger. Overfed, complaisant. And why did your radio promise aid to the freedom fighters of Hungary? Always they said: We are a democracy, too ... I replied in German with an American accent. Who made Germany big and tall? Americans. We have made you strong, with our tax money.

And, little by little, I saw them begin to change. Perhaps because I, too, had become aggressive. Perhaps because ... did they want to be proved wrong?

The first sign of change was in Herbert, the young blond giant. He was still giving orders to the model. Finally I said, as boldly as I could: "Are you in charge here? By whose authority do you change the model?"

He mumbled something.

"In the other studios they go by the clock," I said.

Again the mumble.

Then, from the chapel and the town, the bells sounded. The model looked at me, and before I realized it, I was saying, "Yes, of course, you may change." She did. We went back to work. The buckets of water for our painting had to be carried down a long hallway but all day no one had offered to do the job. I asked quietly, "Do we need some clean water?"

Everyone in the small room heard, but there was no response. I picked up a bucket and struggled out past the five stalwart young men in our group. Returning, I said the only thing I could think of: "Well in America at least, we are not so disrespectful of our elders."

For the first time I caught a glimmer of neighborliness: Katja, a young dark-haired woman, nodded approval. She became my first friend in Kokoschka's castle. At the end of the day she offered to share her locker—one of two in the fortress.

We heard it first on the loudspeaker: Kokoschka, Oskar Kokoschka, and the "last Impressionist." Finally he was coming to his castle on the hill.

We hurried to the courtyard to welcome the man who had brought us—painters, sculptors, art historians and students—from the corners of the earth.

We cheered and clapped as he walked thru the archway. What a picture he made: at 76, a dashing, dapper man with a lively step, a gray crewcut, and darting blue eyes, carrying a red umbrella and a bunch of alpine flowers given him by a child. He was surrounded by an honor guard of seven assistants, the manager of the academy, the local gallery owner, and the tall Olda, his wife. In the excitement of the moment, his eyes were moist with emotion.

He shook hands with students he remembered from other years and told us that this might be his last seminar. He kissed the hands of the Italian princess of Savoy and another young noblewoman (both of whom were enrolled in classes), and then briskly waved everyone back to the studios for inspection and criticism. Each of us had clipped ten or more of his best sketches to his drawing board. As he was to do each day, Kokoschka spent at least an hour in every studio, looking at and commenting on a total of at least 2,000 watercolors a day.

The atmosphere was one of hushed reverence—the kind of subservience I recalled from my school days in Vienna when we sat at attention at our desks and walked on tiptoe between classes. (Then it had seemed natural and fitting; now it was oddly disconcerting ... Suddenly I knew why; I was an American now.)

Yet it was fascinating to watch Kokoschka as he spoke. The mobility of his features, his dynamic gestures, his body waving almost like a dancer's. His mannerisms were calculated to impress his listeners, to make them remember. He was a teacher of great personal magnetism.

He would speak softly about the proper way to observe the model. Then suddenly he would shout the excitement of seeing a light or shadow move across the figure. (This, he was saying, was the adventure of the one and only beautiful moment of a given situation.) He stressed the representation of the space around the form translated into color-spatial concept as opposed to the flat picture plane. He told of his own experiences, quoted poetry (sometimes his own) and described the work of fellow artists and teachers. He was not without prejudice, and he tended to generalize about national characteristics. (American abstract expressionists, by the way, were objects of disdain.)

His coming was always announced on the speakers: "Kokoschka has just entered the building." But he had to tour five floors and often he would sweep unannounced into our studio when we were least prepared. Followed by his swarm of assistants, he would be in the middle of what seemed a fascinating story. He once wrote shocking plays—and designed the stage settings for them. His speech was full of parables.

As a young man (he told us one day) he had traveled in the near east. In Egypt he had visited the tomb of a handsome young pharaoh who held a mirror. The sight inspired him to invent this story: the young pharaoh had married a much older woman who loved him as her own son. After his death the queen had pressed the mirror into his fingers so that each time she visited the tomb she could breathe life into his hand.

Kokoschka compared himself to the queen and us to the pharaoh's mummy. Thru the mirror of art, he said, he was trying to breathe life into our dead hands! For he was the great king-artist, and we were empty pieces of clay. He would open our eyes and teach us to see.

And as it happened, he did. Every day.

He moved from easel to easel. He glanced at some sketches and took a great deal of time with others. He praised lavishly and scolded ruthlessly. His insults were merciless, his criticisms startlingly quick and perceptive. He sifted and compared and, from the work of a few, made selections for exhibition. These sketches were examined again and again each day, and sometimes he exchanged them for better ones by the same artist. The painters whose works were chosen were ecstatic. The others were inspired to work harder, or they wept, in disappointment and despair. (This made me smile, remembering the lesser role of the teacher in America.)

When Kokoschka saw and liked an artist's work, he too, was jubilant. One day I heard him say (in French this time): "Ah this is an artist who has open eyes and an honest, sincere vision—not like that worthless one over there who copies somebody else. Here is someone who is above formula. See—each painting is different, every one fresh. Here is an artist who is thinking! Only an idiot grows up without searching constantly for a fresh outlook."

A moment before I had been trembling when he examined my sketches—trembling like a child. Yet now he was saying this about my work, which was the first to go up on the wall. During rest periods, artists from other studios came to look at our exhibit. "Are you the girl from

Chicago?" they asked me. I began to feel less and less like the ugly American.

During the weeks that followed, that man worked like a dynamo. We each spent ten hours a day, six days a week, in the studios. At dusk, after leaving the castle, a few of us sketched landscapes. (At the end of the seminar, I found I had produced nearly 400 water colors.) And every day rain or shine (and it was more often rain), he would make his way up the mountain by cable car. He preened his amazing memory like a peacock his feathers. He remembered each of us, and he was acutely conscious of the progress and change in our work. Yet he was immensely self-centered, even in informal talks to us.

"I want to leave a legacy of beauty and truth in this, our crazy, rotten world—the beauty that is in the life of everyone, in elusive moments of truth. Go back to your homes all over the world and tell what you have learned here. Show others how to see. I am giving you the last moments of my life because thru you I will live beyond my years ... "

I worked. I went to the splendid festivals with Katja. I saw "Faust" which I had not seen since I was 14, and I felt again (with something like shock) the preoccupation with and reverence for death that was everywhere around me.

One night for the last time I saw Herbert, the blond young giant. He sat down besides me and spoke solemnly. He said he wished I could come to Munich to see more of his work. He said he wished us to be friends. As he spoke, he seemed to be trying to answer his own hard questions:

"I hope my remarks about Americans have not offended you. How do you want us to feel? We had no part in the war—was the war my fault? I am 23. My father was sent to a concentration camp for hiding our family doctor—a Jew. Why do you blame me for what Germany did?"

There were others like him who seemed to hold out their hands in true good will. "Come stay with us, live with us in Germany," they said. "See for yourself that we are not really monsters."

Almost in spite of myself, I began to want to believe them. I could not completely. Not wholly. Yet my bitterness was tempered with wondering. And hope, perhaps.

I had left Austria as a frightened girl, a refugee; I had come back as an American. I had observed at close range one of the greatest living painters—Kokoschka; peasant, actor, businessman, linguist, poet, international charmer, remarkable innovator, and Svengali. I had finished a chapter in my own life—a chapter of longing for the country of my birth, and now I was returning to the country of my choice.

No, I will not soon forget summer in Salzburg, now that I am truly home again.

November 14th 1964

The Chicago Daily News printed my story of: *Reflections of an artist's life in Vienna, London and Chicago, an immigrant's Odyssey*, and winning the prestigious prize of "*Outstanding Achievement in the field of Art, by an American citizen of foreign birth*" I felt very humble in the company of my fellow prize winners in various fields and from countries around the world. At the Awards dinner at the Ambassador East, I was seated next to the famous cartoonists Al Capp (Li'l Abner), Chester Gould (Dick Tracy), Milton Caniff (Steve Canyon) Allen Saunders (Mary Worth), who handed out the awards. My family sat in the audience at a table with our friends. The Immigrant's Service League, who gives out these yearly awards, was founded by Jane Adams in 1908.

Paul

The wind off the lake drove the raindrops into vertical strings, making the highway slippery. As I drove, the windshield wiper left streaks on the glass.

Surely Paul's flight was delayed due to weather but I could not count on that. How will he be able to find me unless I am standing at the gate in my new hat I asked myself? I missed the entrance to the parking structure, which meant driving all the way around the airport again.

Would he be as handsome as the last time I saw him, with blond hair wavy and unruly, bright blue eyes with a roguish twinkle in them? Was he still slender as well as tall? What luck—there was a place to park my station wagon, not always an easy feat at O'Hare Airport, supposedly the busiest airport in the country. The clock on my dashboard showed six-thirty p.m. and the flight from Washington D.C. was due at six-forty-eight p.m. What a relief! I felt good in my wine-colored outfit, which I had assembled yesterday at Marshall Field's. My mink hat matched the fur collar on my Alaskan seal coat. Although I'd made it to the airport in time, I would still have to run if I were to be at the Delta gate in time to greet Paul.

So many thoughts were racing through my head, and I asked myself, "What am I doing here?" My twenty-one-year marriage to Charley was good, but here I was, meeting a married man, albeit an old friend from my long distant past. Why was Paul coming all this way to see me? Neither of us brought our spouses to this reunion, nor did we tell them about it. The note I had left for Charley said that my closest friend Claudy had asked me to come and spend the afternoon and night with her in Wilmette. I indicated that she had a problem and needed me for moral support.

Lots of people carrying luggage were streaming into the waiting area. Flight 821 had arrived. My stomach was alive with butterflies; my temples were beginning to race like my thumping heart. Was this the reaction of a grown woman of forty-one or a teenage groupie?

There! I recognized Paul, nicely dressed, not much taller than me, white hair, suntanned, the same light blue eyes, not so slender and with a slight limp. For a moment, I felt like turning and running. "Hilda," he said in that wonderful, resonant, familiar voice, and pinched my cheek. He stepped back and looked at me, flashing that charming smile. "You are so pretty!"

His reservation was at the Ambassador East, and he said that we could have dinner at the Pump Room or anywhere I chose.

"You look very well, Paul. It is so good to see you after such a long time. Where did you get that tan? Before we decide on anything, why don't we go to my car and we'll talk?"

I hoped it all sounded natural and did not show my rattled nerves. It was cold as we walked to the parking structure, but the rain had stopped

Paul said "Mina, the children and I, just got back from the Bahamas, where Mina's brother has a house. It so happened that I had the opportunity to look at a plant for sale here in Chicago, which makes my visit easy to explain. You know I have twin boys, they are my pride and joy."

We were at the car, and as I fumbled with the key, I hoped Paul didn't notice that I was trembling. He held the door open for me as I slid into the driver's seat. He walked around the car and got in on the passenger side.

"Paul, it is rather awkward for me to go downtown and have dinner with a gentleman in a very popular restaurant when I am supposed to be visiting a friend."

He smiled, touched my hand, and moved closer. "That's no problem—I'll cancel my reservation at the Ambassador and we can just go to the Hilton right here at the airport if that would make you feel more comfortable." His hand left mine with a gentle squeeze as he reached for my shoulder and pulled me toward him. "We didn't even say a proper hello," he whispered. He kissed me gently on the mouth. His lips were soft and sweet.

He pulled off my hat and took my face in his hands, and I could smell a lovely cologne or shaving lotion, his face now close to mine.

He was quite wrinkled but still handsome at age 54. He suddenly burst out laughing. "Hilda, dear Hilda—you look like a scared bunny rabbit. I am not going to bite you. We are going to relax and enjoy each other. Put your defenses down and let your natural charm take over."

He sat back and smiled as I started the car. Because it was so cold, it took three tries to get the motor going. There was a lot of traffic, and it took all of my concentration to maneuver into the correct lane. As I drove, Paul's leg was very close to mine, and I felt a surge of warmth going through my entire body.

It started to snow very wet snowflakes. As I fumbled to start the wipers, a silly old ditty came to my mind. "Windshield wiper, *sh, sh.*" When we arrived at the Airport Hilton, Paul jumped out of the car, came to my side, and held the door for me while taking my left hand in his. Mine was cold as ice and his was warm and comforting.

As we walked toward the check-in counter, I said, "I'll wait for you here," and I sat down in a dimmer area of the lobby between a potted plant and a marble pillar. When Paul came back, he said, "Let's go upstairs so I can clean up and shave. We'll have some champagne and *hors d'oeuvres* before we go and have dinner in the Sky Room. The concierge says they have a fine chanteuse. Does that suit you? Here is the room key—if you would like to go up first, I'll follow in a minute or so after I order room service."

He was being very perceptive about my nervousness and he seemed experienced at clandestine meetings. He handed me one of two room keys, and like a robot I headed for the bank of elevators. The room was on the eighth floor, and it was beautiful. It was really a suite. There was a nice Monet print of Giverny over the sofa and a Seurat Grande Jatte print hung over the bed while some Paul Klees were clustered in the little foyer. The room's décor was elegant and relaxing. My coat and hat were still wet, so I put them into the hall closet.

Now I wondered where to seat myself—the chair or the sofa?

The door opened and Paul walked in, threw his coat on a chair, looked around and nodded. "Nice, don't you think?" He excused himself and disappeared into the bathroom, just before a waiter arrived at our room with a tray of little open faced sandwiches, an ice bucket and a bottle of champagne.

From behind the bathroom door, Paul called out, "Hilda, if it is our refreshments, please have the man open the wine for us. I'll be out in a second." The waiter popped the cork and foam bubbled on the carpet. Paul emerged, indeed refreshed, and he tipped the waiter and escorted him out.

Paul raised his glass. "Now, a toast to our reunion after—how many years is it? Do you remember how we toasted such an occasion in Vienna?"

"Paul, I must admit that I've never had such an occasion before, neither in Vienna nor in the United States. You mean a seduction scene, or the linking of arms and toasting the shedding of the formal German *Sie* and instead substituting the informal *Du?*"

He burst out laughing when I asked him that. The man oozed charm and I could feel myself being captivated by him all over again as I took a sip of champagne, the perfect libation for a nondrinker like me. He poured himself a second glass as we sat down on the couch and let the moment linger. After a short silence, he said, "Now we have to fill in all the blanks of the past twenty-five years or so since we last saw each other."

We had spoken over the telephone several times since Mrs. Mandel had retrieved his number in Washington D.C., but it was different now that we were face to face.

"When I got over the wonderful surprise of hearing from you, I could only picture the little girl in my grandfather's garden. You were a chubby little thing with rosy cheeks and you always ran toward me to say hello. I watched you grow into a lovely young woman, tall and beautiful, intelligent, and knowledgeable about many subjects, wise beyond your age. I remember that you always had a funny story to tell when I gave you a ride, and you also asked me a lot of questions. Even though you were just a child in my eyes, I felt free to talk to you about my girlfriend Toni, and my reluctance to marry Mina."

He leaned over and gave me a peck on the cheek, took a little sandwich, leaned back and looked at me intensely, his mouth curling into that bemused, ubiquitous smile.

I told him of my escape from Austria, and how pleased I was to learn in London that he had been freed from Dachau—as a result of Mina's bravery.

There was more conversation, and Paul said; though recalling that part of our lives was terribly important, it was not what we should be thinking about tonight.

"I suggest that you now take a deep breath and have a bite to eat and a glass of champagne," he told me. "I want this to be a very sweet way of making us come closer together; like two old friends finding a new kind of bond. You are lovelier than I had imagined, a successful artist, a great part of my past life and youth. It is difficult for me to restrain my impulse, to seduce you right here and now. But everything, everything that this evening brings will have to happen with you setting the pace. Though I find you utterly charming, you obviously are not completely comfortable with this fascinating, strange and unbelievable reunion. Since we must be downstairs in half an hour, may I now kiss you, not like a stranger, but someone whom, as you have confessed to me, you have loved and thought about since you were five years old?"

When we entered the Sky Room, the musicians started to play a Viennese waltz. No doubt, Paul had arranged for that. He guided me to the dance floor. With his arms around me, the music and the two glasses of champagne, my dream had come true.

Snow White, Juliet, Heloise, Cleopatra and every movie star—their romances shrank into oblivion. My euphoria and enchantment defied description. Paul's breath brushed my ear, his cheek close to mine, his skin silken after his shave. He said. "Now, I recall dancing with you at my wedding in the Hotel Bristol ballroom in Vienna."

I too had thought about that time, how terribly hurt and disappointed I was that I was not the bride at the wedding. Despite his limp, he danced well and now held me securely as we reversed and turned faster and faster. "Roses of the South" was a familiar waltz to me. I had danced to it in Vienna in 1933 in Madame Suschitzky's children's dance troupe. We performed on stage of the wonderful new Movie Palace called the Scala near our home in Vienna. Dancing here with Paul was like a film playing in my head in full color, bringing back my childhood. We laughed a lot and congratulated each other on our dance performance. The Chanteuse sang 1940's songs like, "All the things you are."

My guilt feelings vanished. Surely I was entitled to turn my lifelong fantasy and longing into reality.

Over dinner, I told him about Oskar Kokoschka, with whom Papa had gone to school at the beginning of the twentieth century. I told him how Charley had encouraged me to attend the seminar and not miss the chance to study with such a famous painter and a countryman to boot. I told him how subsequently the Fairweather Hardin Gallery in Chicago had shown some of the 350 watercolors I had produced in Salzburg under Kokoschka's direction. I told him many things before he guided me back to his room.

I took a deep breath, reached for both his hands, looked into his blue eyes and said: "It's very difficult for me to say, but all my life I have prided myself on my honesty and loyalty. I needed Charley to help my parents. He is the most generous, gentlest, loving, honest man. How can I now commit adultery, even though the temptation is so great? I confess that I have never stopped loving you, comparing every man I met with you, dreaming of you and fantasizing about you, ever since I was five years old. And now being charmed and thrilled by you, it is as if my dream has come true. I am afraid I must get my coat and leave here now."

He extricated his hands from mine, and took me in his arms. He kissed my ears, my neck, my mouth. "Don't think of this as adultery. This is the dream come true, yours and mine. My marriage was forced upon me; you are everything I could ever long for. Mina and I have nothing in common, except the love for our wonderful children. My debt to her is one of the greatest gratitude, which I express over and over. She and my sister Trude surely saved me from torture and death in Dachau. You owe Charley equal gratitude for getting your parents out of England during the war. But, you and I owe each other the joy and pleasure of this wonderful night."

I did not have the chance to answer him. He kept kissing me gently, holding me close. My body was on fire.

Yet I could not go through with this dream of my lifelong passionate fairy tale. "Darling Paul, please don't be angry with me. Try to understand that I have to be the person I am."

He stepped back, looked at me long and hard, walked to a chair, pulled out a cigar, lit it and puffed slowly. Finally he said: "It was a long way from Washington to Chicago just to take you out to dinner. I am surprised and disappointed." I spent the night at my friend Claudy's.

Some days later I received a letter from Paul, which I kept in my pocket until I could find a safe place to read it at home before I would have to leave for the train station to pick up Charley.

Dear Hilda,

"Things have been hectic at my plant ever since I got back here. My foreman quit his job and we have been looking to replace him. The business I had looked at in Chicago was not what I had expected. The big government order we are working on won't be ready as scheduled and that means a lot of trouble ahead, maybe even the loss of a future order ... "

By this time I found big teardrops on the paper. I had expected a passionate love letter and not a business report. The entire page had more details of all his problems. It was hand printed in very clear and neat lettering. He went on to tell me about his twin boys, their school, their various activities and the camps they were considering for the coming summer. A second page told about his plans to go to a spa in Florida the following month. His wife did not like it there, so he was going there alone

... " I would much rather talk to you on the phone, but I don't suppose you would want me to call you. I'll wait for your reply." In haste,

Paul.

So, he was asking me to come to him in Florida. Obviously he was not demonstrative in writing, perhaps because he didn't want any written record. Perhaps I was being overly romantic. What did I really want? Was I now ready to have an affair with him and betray Charley? I reread the letter, ripped it into little pieces and buried it in the garbage. It made me laugh.

My intimacy with my husband had become more loving and attentive since my rendezvous with Paul. All the many years of making an idol of Paul, thinking of him, dreaming of him, wishing for him and comparing every man with him, made my realization of those fantasies seem my right. But now I could see that my idol's feet had some clay on them.

Global Adventure with Charley

With Diana in college, the opportunity presented itself of taking an extended vacation with Charley. I had been fascinated much of my life by the Orient, especially its art, but never had been there. Now Pan Am had a promotional around-the-world fare of $1,200 per person, with unlimited stopovers, so long as one kept traveling in the same general direction.

Charley and I studied maps, marked various cities, looked up tours, and read up on such world famous hotels as the one designed by Frank Lloyd Wright in Tokyo, the Myako in Kyoto, and the Raffles in Singapore. We factored in palaces in India, famous hotels Ceylon, Thailand, Cambodia and Bali. And we figured we would skip over the Middle East and fly directly to Rome, then to Paris, and on home to Chicago. We penciled in, crossed out, and re-penciled destinations, eventually creating an odysscy that would last six weeks.

"Six weeks?" said Charley, incredulous.

"Please, let's do it now, while we are young enough to enjoy it," I pleaded.

There was so much to see and remember, but the stories I want to share with you took place in Kyoto and in New Delhi

From the lovely Myako Hotel we took a bus to what we thought was the center of Kyoto. We asked the driver if he spoke English. He said yes. We came to a bus stop that looked busy and we asked if this was the stop for Takashimaya, a department store. I was looking for woolen socks, because you had to take off your shoes in temples and it was freezing cold with only the paper slippers they gave you. Told "yes," we got off the bus but could not find Takashimaya. We stopped in a small store to ask directions. The people indicated they did not speak English but gestured for us to sit down and wait while a man got us help.

Soon he came back with another man who bowed to us and said he spoke English and would take us to Takashimaya. After we arrived, the nice man translated to three sales ladies in white smocks what I wanted. This produced much whispering and agitation, until finally they explained to our volunteer guide what the problem was. He wrung his hand, obviously quite embarrassed. At long last, he said to me. "Madame I don't know how to tell you and I hope you will not feel that I am insulting you, will you therefore forgive me in advance. Unfortunately there are no socks in the ladies department that would fit your feet. We will have to go to the men's department, if you have no objection. It is really a great dilemma for us to have to inconvenience you like this."

Charley and I almost laughed out loud. But we remained serious and I said, "Please think nothing of it. I know that my feet are larger than the delicate Japanese ladies' feet. Let us go to the men's department." So, the guide went with us and I found warm socks.

The guide joined us for dinner at a restaurant where the seating arrangements were most uncomfortable. We had to sit on a cushion on the floor and our legs were dangling in a sort of pit, with a table growing out of it. The food was excellent. Our friend asked a lot of questions about my work and Charley's and I told about an artist friend in Chicago who was Japanese with whom I had exhibited in several art shows. Our new friend asked if he could take our picture. After dinner he insisted on taking us back to our hotel. He had spent five hours with us. We thanked him profusely. In Japan tipping is not accepted, which I think is great.

The next morning as we went for breakfast, several people came up to us in the hotel breakfast room. One woman asked, "Are you the famous artist from Chicago?" I replied that I was from Chicago and that I paint but that I was not a famous artist.

"Oh, but your photo is on the front page of the *Mainichi Daily Times* with a long article about you." She said. We were astounded and incredulous and quickly bought the paper. Sure enough there was my picture and the article obviously written by our volunteer guide. Everything I had told him was misquoted or turned around in such a way as to give an entirely false meaning. But my name was spelled right.

We arrived in New Delhi in time for a celebration of Indian Independence. People in their national dress arrived in busloads from all over India, and even Princess Anne of England was there. One man whom we met on the tour bus, turned out to be Aspee, a Bombay-born architect and engineer who lived in Florida and Europe with his American wife. A Zoroaster Parsee, he had come to his native land to visit his aged and ailing father. Aspee translated for us whenever we wanted to converse with other Indians who could not speak English. We asked permission to take their pictures, and some had never seen a camera before. Nor had some of the women ever seen nylon stockings, and, through Aspee, they asked if they could touch my legs. I discreetly took off my stockings and gave them to one villager, who screeched with delight.

From the Indian capital, we were supposed to catch a flight to Agra in order to see the Taj Mahal, but the fog was so dense our plane could not take off. So we decided to take a taxi for the forty-mile trip. "Do you speak English?" we asked the driver. "Yes," he said. We agreed upon a price and got in the cab. Later we realized that his "yes" was the only English word he knew.

We drove for an hour before coming to a railroad crossing. The bar was down and we had to wait for the train. Suddenly the driver exited the cab, leaving us to sit there. No train came, but plenty of children did—all of them begging. I gave them small change from my coin purse, then my lipstick, then my hanky, and more and more children came, followed by women with babies, other adults, crippled men, and some people who had lost fingers to leprosy. My purse was now empty.

We closed the windows, and fifty or more people in rags surrounded us, some climbing onto the roof of our car. Charley, normally unafraid of anything, started to worry for our lives. We had no weapons. We felt so rich and they had nothing. They might kill us to get our clothes and our wallets. We had given them money and had only enough left for our trip and nothing over that. It was beastly hot inside the car.

Norman Cousins had coined a phrase "compassion fatigue" and that is what we felt at that time. At first our hearts went out to the poor little children who came and begged. Then the adults started coming and we felt so sorry for them and were overwhelmed with compassion seeing their rags and their crippled fingers and disease-ridden faces. However, when they came in large numbers and climbed on the roof of the taxi we began to get angry and afraid and were worried about our own safety. Gone was the feeling of compassion replaced by fear, I am sad to say. I started to think of all the possessions we and everyone we knew was burdened with back home. While here the poverty and misery was overwhelming and pervasive. How could we help such huge numbers of destitute people, some wearing rags that used to be rags? Charley and I held on to each other and I cried.

Finally, after one hour, the driver came back, wordlessly lifted the bar by the railroad tracks and we went on. The train never came. It was all a trick. We were furious but what could we do? Eventually, there was Agra and the fabulous Taj Mahal. It had rained the night before; everything was still wet and sparkling in the sun. We quickly forgot about our ordeal and reveled in the story and the exquisite beauty of the Taj Mahal, which was a monument to love. At the reflection pool, there was Aspee, who told us he had taken the train from New Delhi without incident. If only we had known there was a train.

Because our flight to Rome had been delayed, we all were sent to a hotel where we were awakened by ringing phones at four a.m. We saw Aspee again at the airport, and when they finally canceled the flight to Rome, we decided to go to Paris instead. Aspee turned out to have tickets on that flight. By that time we were good buddies. While in the air, the plane's instruments showed a problem with the landing gear, forcing us to make an emergency landing in Teheran, which the pilot did safely with just a big bump. While the problem was still unsolved after several hours, we were sent to a different hotel, where Aspee joined us for dinner. He ordered a sensational meal for us, which unfortunately made us ill hours later. But we soldiered on. While Charley and Aspee went for a walk, I found a beauty shop to have my hair done. The ladies of Teheran liked to do up their thick black hair in very ornate hairdos. Except for the fact that the towel around my neck was dirty and wet, I was impressed by the knowledge and skill of the hair dressers.

We returned to the Teheran airport eighteen hours after arriving, only to find that the plane still was awaiting a shipment of parts from Europe. Aspee decided we should not take a chance on the Iranian repair people. An experienced negotiator and travel guide par excellence, he arranged for our tickets to be switched to another airline. There still was the problem of the luggage, however; Aspee and Charley ran out on the tarmac, climbed into the belly of the plane, found our luggage and carried it back while two soldiers pointed guns at them, apparently ready to shoot. I clung to the guards, crying and screaming for help and mercy. How the three of us got onto the other airplane, I cannot recall. I was so emotionally exhausted; I was shaking like the proverbial leaf.

In Paris, we separated from our new friend. He flew on to Miami and we went to Philadelphia to see Diana at the University of Pennsylvania. We promised Aspee to visit him in Miami, and he promised to come see us in Chicago. Our friendship, formed in adversity, has lasted more than forty-five years and will continue to the end of our lives. Our love for him has extended to his new Danish wife Grethe, and to their son, Alistair, who is my godson. Aspee and Grethe have collected my paintings. We see each other all too seldom, but feel close to each other nonetheless.

When Charley and I arrived in Philly, it was snowing and the snow was deep. Traffic was at a standstill and there was not a snowplough in sight. The Warwick Hotel, which we had telephoned from New York to confirm our reservations, turned out to be full up. After twenty-five hours on a plane and a train, I told the room clerk that I would collapse right in front of him if he did not find me accommodations immediately. We opened the closet door of the room we were shown, and there was a man still inside. I believe he was equally as startled as we were.

We telephoned Diana, who was thrilled to hear from us, but there was no way to reach her except on foot. I didn't dare risk it; I didn't have sufficiently warm clothes for such an excursion, but Charley decided to walk there anyway. Two hours later, he called from her dorm room. The entire time he walked and walked he met only one man, whom he asked for directions. The man said, "I am from the

Sudan and I don't know my way around either." Somehow Charley made his way to Diana.

Traffic started to move again the next day and we spent two delightful days with our wonderful girl. Soon afterwards she graduated from the Wharton School of Finance and set out for a career in New York.

Life cycles

Diana made the rounds of the Wall Street brokerage houses in an effort to find a job. If they knew what we knew about her lifelong fascination with the stock market, they would have hired her in a minute. But it seemed Diana was ahead of her time; none of the brokerage houses wanted to hire a woman in 1963.

She did land a job with IBM, they sent her to New Jersey on a three-month training program, after which she had to pass a very difficult test. She became a systems analyst with a specialty in time-sharing. At the time, computers were huge machines and too expensive for use by just one company.

More importantly, Everett Daly, a tall and handsome young man, also worked at IBM. And they fell in love.

Charley and I gave them a beautiful wedding in December 1968 at the Arts Club of Chicago followed by a honeymoon in Hawaii. It was a happy time for all of us. They both had good jobs and were very much in love. They found a lovely apartment in Manhattan.

We decided to sell our home in Highland Park and move to a twenty-sixth-floor apartment close to downtown Chicago. This enabled me to walk to the Art Institute of Chicago and Charley to drive to work in just ten minutes. Mutti happily settled not far from us in a senior residence, where she had lots of company and many interesting activities.

Urban living differed considerably from the suburban. Bijou our poodle, missed roaming freely in the woods and ravines of Highland Park, and had to get used to going up and down on elevators and walking on a leash. We enjoyed easy access to plays and concerts. The management of our building allowed me to conduct art classes in the community room on the penthouse floor. Some of my students from Highland Park, Deerfield and other suburbs came into the city to attend my classes. Life was good. .

One morning, my powerful and strong Charley did one hundred pushups and said to me: "Hilda touch my arms and chest, see how tough I am." He was in top physical shape. On a hot and humid August day of 1969 we loaded the station wagon to take my paintings to the Art Fair in No-Man's Land. Getting all the props together and then setting up in the village square was a herculean effort. But sales were good and it was worth it.

Charley went for ice-cream, after he was gone for what seemed to be a very long time, I asked Fred, a family friend, to see if he could find Charley. Perhaps he was visiting with the other artists or maybe sitting in the car listening to a Chicago Cubs game. Ten minutes later, Fred returned and told me that Charley was slumped over the steering wheel in the car with the doors locked. I ran to the car while Fred and Stella watched my paintings.

Opening the door, I found Charley in pain, feeling very cold to the touch, but complaining that he was hot. Leaning on my horn, I started to drive to Evanston Hospital, hoping the police would stop me. They soon did and summoned an ambulance. Charley refused to get on a stretcher, making it a point to climb into the passenger seat of the Fire Department ambulance.

They took Charley to Chicago's Illinois Masonic Hospital,s emergency room. Our regular doctor was on vacation, and I had to telephone the doctor on call.

Charley was dead by the time I got back to him. I could not believe it. Why couldn't the five interns have helped him? My own heart almost stopped. This strong wonderful man, who was never sick a day in his life, who in our twenty-eight years together, never even had a cold, how could it be? Just that day he looked so suntanned and athletic in the blue polo shirt. Diana had just given it to him two weeks before, for his sixty-fourth birthday. He must only have fallen asleep. Surely he would wake up. He couldn't be dead. I started to shake him awake, but the nurses pulled me away and walked me to the waiting room.

I sat down there and cried and cried. A doctor came to talk to me and asked me a lot of questions.

Then I had to drive back to the Art Fair and tell my friends what had happened. It was a surrealistic scene as we went about the commonplace task of loading my paintings back into the car, then unloading them at my home. Fred and Stella offered to stay over-night, I thanked them but said that I needed to be alone.

I called Mutti and then Diana in New York, to tell them the tragic news. Diana and Everett immediately booked a flight from New York to Chicago. Mutti wanted to spend the night with me, but I asked her not to come. I needed time to think, time to accept the truth. I could not squelch my resentment over the fact that there was no American doctor in the ER, that the young Asian, Indian and Arab interns had no idea how to keep Charley alive. My head was splitting with grief and rage.

I knew I had to pull myself together because arrangements had to be made. This was neither the time for self-pity nor for blaming the hospital staff. My inner voice helped me use my common sense. Just six months before we had made out new wills and had purchased cemetery plots next to the one in which Papa was buried. We also had joined a burial society that would handle all the funeral details.

My intention was to have a small funeral at the mortuary, but so many people came that they had to use a much larger hall. Charley was so loved and respected.

Mutti, Diana and I felt lost and devastated. Friends came daily to be with us, offering help, bringing loads of food. Some nights twenty or thirty people would arrive and stay for several hours. Our table was set as if for a banquet, and it seemed there was a party every night. Eventually, Diana and her husband returned to New York. I resumed teaching my art classes, and Mutti helped keep the apartment in order. On the surface, life had returned to normal—except that I felt I had been cut in half.

I refused invitations for evenings. All I wanted to do was sit in Charley's chair and cry. I begged Mutti to return to her own home at the senior complex. It was better for me not to have to pretend how strong I was. For the first time in my life I lost my appetite. I lost weight without even trying. I stopped painting. I felt I could never paint again.

How does one learn to be a widow? Charley was my rock. It seemed my strength had dissolved in tears. Only from exhaustion would I fall asleep after midnight, and I would beat the sun up. How could sunrise over Lake Michigan be so beautiful when Charley was not here to share it with me?

The Road to Recovery

Diana came to visit me for a weekend in January 1970. I cooked all her favorite foods for dinner. We sat down, two of us next to the empty chair. My friend Anne telephoned to say that she had tickets for a charity dinner and play at the Ivanhoe Theater. She would be at my door in ten minutes.

"Oh, I could not possibly go, Diana is here for the first time in five months since Charley died, and I don't go out at night yet," I informed her.

"Nonsense," she said, then hung up.

A few minutes later, she was at my door. I had to let her in. She was determined not to take no for an answer. "Diana, don't you think you'd enjoy dinner and a play? Wouldn't it be good for your mother to get out? Isn't it time for her to stop being a hermit?"

Diana took her side. "Mom, she is right. And, I would love to go, so you have to do that for my sake."

Anne spoke about how there would be various people from the art world there, including the director of the Museum of Contemporary Art, a well-known art critic, and some artists I would know. If necessary, she said, I could think of it as a business development outing. Outnumbered and out-argued, I gave in.

Our doorman got us a cab, and we arrived in less formal attire than the occasion called for. Diana engaged in pleasant conversations, while I kept hoping no one would ask me about Charley, or, if they knew, comment on his loss. I was afraid I would again dissolve into tears. The dimming lights announced it was time to go to the little theatre. Diana and I were seated on one side of the round stage; Anne was seated on another with two gentlemen of her acquaintance.

Neither Diana nor I found ourselves enjoying "The Little Foxes," so, following the first act, we sought to excuse ourselves. "Anne dear, it was so nice of you to invite us," I said. "We did enjoy the dinner, but we are leaving now. The play is not right for us at this time, I hope you understand." To the two gentlemen, one of whom was quite good looking, I said: "It was nice to meet you."

The good-looking one asked if, instead of our leaving, he could buy me a drink at the bar downstairs. "I'm not really enjoying the play either, and Two-Ton Baker is at the Piano Bar. It would cheer us up." Furthermore, he said, the way it was snowing outside, it would be difficult to get a cab until later. So why not join him, and he also could get a bite to eat, having missed dinner.

Good looking and charming, I thought. "All right, you convinced me, if you will also include my daughter in your invitation," I replied.

Anne did not seem pleased by this development. However, she suggested that after the play concluded we rendezvous at the main exit. Diana was delighted at the prospect of seeing Two-Ton Baker, whom she used to watch performing on television when she was little. He was such fun when he played the piano while jumping on the bench and pounding the keys.

Our new host turned out to be named Norm Pierce. Play-acting as if I were not in the room, he said to Diana: "Your mother is very cute. Do you think she would go out with me?"

"Lord knows she is old enough. Why don't you ask her yourself?" responded my tactful girl.

"Would you, Hilda?" he smiled. His voice was very melodious.

"I have not been on a date for more than twenty-eight years, I don't think I would know how to act," I stalled.

"Of course you would, it's like riding a bike. You never forget how, even if you haven't done it for awhile."

Two-ton inadvertently came to my rescue. "Norm, old pal, how goes it?" he asked, without taking his hands off the piano keys. Introductions were made and Diana seemed so excited. I ordered a discreet Perrier with lime, prompting Norm to laugh. He ordered Tanqueray Gin for himself and another for Two-Ton, who was aptly named. He was a huge man. Diana had a glass of wine.

We chatted and laughed a lot, something I had not done for months, and it felt good. Norm was so easy to talk to; it was like having an instant friend. It turned out he had been a radio and television announcer and was the founder of "The Music Lovers Hour" of classical music on WIND radio. Now he produced training films for the Food Industry. The time passed so quickly and pleasantly, we had to rush through the crowd to meet Anne and our driver her friend Jack.

Huge snowflakes floated slowly down to the sidewalk. Our feet got soaked as we were in nylons and high heels. Luckily the car was at the curb. Anne got dropped off first. Diana sat up front with Jack, leaving Norm and me in the back seat. Very quickly, it seemed, we were at our building. Norm jumped out of the car, walked Diana and me to the door. We thanked Jack and said good night to Norm as he held the entrance door open for us. Norm again asked me if he could call me. I nodded agreement.

By the time we had shaken out our coats, hung them on the shower rod to dry, and peeled off our wet panty hose, the telephone rang. It was Norm.

"I'd like to take you both out to breakfast tomorrow morning," he said in that nice voice of his.

"Unfortunately, Diana has to catch an early flight to New York and I am invited to brunch at a friend's," I answered honestly.

"Okay, how about dinner?"

Again I was truthful. "I must take down a show of my work and my friends promised to help me load them into my car and take them up to my apartment, which is a huge chore."

"Well," he said, "it seems you are too hard to get, which I truly regret."

"I am not playing hard to get. I'll tell you what, let me call my friends and ask if I may bring you along. I'll call you back if they agree."

Stella was delighted that I would bring an escort. As matters turned out, Norm knew most of the people at the brunch and had a great time.

He offered to help me take down my show. My friend Fred was happy to get off the hook. Norm was a great help and very admiring of my paintings. He carefully loaded the car. We had dinner at the Pancake House across the street from the exhibition and it was midnight by the time each painting was finally hanging back in its place in my home.

Before leaving, Norm invited me to lunch with him on Wednesday and for dinner with him on Saturday night. I accepted the invitation for Wednesday, but explained that I would be leaving on Saturday for Los Angeles, where I would board a cruise ship to teach painting to my fellow passengers. A friend who had purchased one of my paintings some years before was now cruise director on the ship. The friend, whom I will call Lisa, had telephoned from Milan, Italy and said I could have a free two-week roundtrip cruise to Mexico in return for teaching three one-hour-long classes per week. I had accepted with thanks, thinking that was the way to finally end my self-pity and grieving.

"If you let me I will be glad to drive you and your mother to the airport Saturday and pick you up when you return," Norm said when we were having dinner at my home. Mutti was planning to fly to New York to visit with Diana for a while. I was very pleased with Norm's offer, and gladly accepted.

That's when he kissed me—gently—and left. Wow! As tired as I was, I could not fall asleep after that kiss. After a hot bath and dressed in my warm robe, I went to the living room and sat on the couch looking out at the lights of the city.

Wednesday lunch was very nice. The Shish kebab restaurant on Rush Street was a small intimate place just a short walk from my home. I realized that Norm had a striking resemblance to Danny Kaye, only with gray hair. He wore his tweedy sport coat with ease and his button-down yellow striped shirt looked good with that jacket.

He greeted me with a grin, and two outstretched hands. "You look grand with that mink hat, and even better in broad daylight than last Sunday night!" he said. "Have you eaten here before? No? You'll enjoy their home cooking. At least it's great home cooking for me.

My mother was a rotten cook. Does a fine artist like you like to cook?"

I felt immediately comfortable, as if I had known him forever. I really, really liked him. I was charmed by the way he could draw people out without seeming overly inquisitive. He was attentive, interested, and interesting.

A number of people stopped at our table to greet him and exchange a few words. Without being rude or arrogant, he indicated to them that perhaps he and they could chat another time, because he was under some time pressure to get back to work and he and I had some things to talk over before then. He was shooting a film for the food industry, and had a photographer and grip waiting for him.

"May I call you tonight if ten-thirty isn't too late, so we can talk some more?" he asked as he started to rise. "I hate to run off so soon, but I loved having lunch with you. Thank you so much for coming," he added. We shook hands. I thanked him in turn, and told him he could indeed call me. As we walked in different directions, I thought that on the near north side of Chicago, everything is in proximity, so it's easy and fun to walk everywhere.

After getting home, I received a call from Anne. "Has Jack called you for a date yet?"

"Uh, Jack?"

"He's a very wealthy plumbing contractor," she said, going on to tell me that she and Norm had been childhood friends, and that when they went on that theatre date, she had thought maybe Jack would be perfect for me.

"Ummm, Norm and I just had lunch," I told her.

"Oh, for heaven's sake, don't fall for him because he is such a well-known radio and TV personality. He's dated every divorcee and widow up and down Lake Shore Drive. He'll drop you like a hot potato if you don't succumb to his advances very quickly. So don't be a fool and mess with him."

I thanked her for her advice, telling her I needed to get to the art class I was teaching upstairs.

My students had become my family. Their love and respect helped me more than anything else after my shattering loss.

Helen, whose husband was a respected Justice of the Illinois Supreme Court, had commissioned me to do a large painting for their church in Park Ridge. Even though I protested that I had not touched a brush since my father's and husband's funerals, they insisted that I go to the Lincoln Park Zoo near the seal's exhibit to paint a landscape including the charming turn-of-the-century refreshment stand. They wanted to hang it in the children's play-room of their church. The judge in particular was quite persuasive with his arguments, so I relented. Getting back to my career and normal busy life would be therapeutic.

Suddenly, it seemed, other friends commissioned new paintings for their homes, or came to my studio to buy some of my work. I was truly touched by their warmth and kindness.

There was another woman also named Helen in my class. Like my own paintings, her collages were accepted at the Art Rental and Sales Gallery of the Art Institute of Chicago. She gave me her seventh-row center Thursday night seats at the Chicago Symphony.

That night I woke up at ten-thirty p.m. to the sound of the phone ringing. "Hilda, did I wake you?" Norm asked with concern.

I confessed that I had snoozed, but was wide awake now. I enjoyed talking with him for some forty-five minutes. He told me about the day's shoot, and also about his past work as the voice of "The Music Lover's Hour."

"On hot nights, before air-conditioning was in all cars, Charley and I used to drive to the North Shore to cool off, park by the lake, listen to your music and smooch," I told him.

He laughed, saying many people had told him his music had touched off their romances. "I'll see you Saturday, but that seems like such a long way off," he said. "I'm working downtown again tomorrow and could break away for a short lunch at Marshall Fields, or how about Toffenetti's? They might have faster service. I'll be finished with this job by the time you come back from your cruise, and then I'll have time to properly entertain you and your mother."

That did not sound like the person Anne had cautioned me about. Norm and I met Thursday and Friday for lunch, and Saturday he came to help me. He carried my luggage to the car and we drove north to pick up Mutti. She seemed to like him right away. As her flight to New York left one hour after mine, Norm offered to stay with her and see her to her gate.

When I telephoned her from Los Angeles, she informed me: "That is the man you will marry. I can tell by the way you look at each other."

"Mutti, what a ridiculous thing to say! I just met the man this week."

She giggled and handed the phone to Diana, her favorite (only) granddaughter, with whom she would be sightseeing for the entire week.

"My mother, the popular teenager," Diana greeted me. I told her that Norm had given me one yellow rose at the airport and had kissed my hand.

"Mother, you know what a yellow rose means? It's flower talk for "I love you.""

"Nonsense," I replied. "How would he know a thing like that? I don't know it. Stop teasing me, you two!"

"Ask any florist, Mom. Happy romance."

"You should be more respectful of your old mother," I scolded her. Now, show Mutti a good time, but don't wear her out. She's seventy-nine years old. I love you and will miss you terribly."

They wished me *bon voyage*, and I reminded them that Norm would be waiting for Mutti when she returned to Chicago, and that both of them thereafter would come to meet my flight from Los Angeles.

Aboard the Princess Italia

Very early one morning I received a call from Milan, Italy. It was Lisa, who after she had bought one of my paintings had invited us to a big party in her home in Highland Park. Since then we had become good friends. "Hilda I have something exciting to tell you. I am coming to the states on a new Cruise ship and we would like to have you come on the inaugural cruise out of Los Angeles down the Mexican Riviera and back again. You would be required to teach three art classes of one hour duration for each of the two weeks. I will be the Cruise Director in charge of all the entertainment. How does that sound to you?"

Without hesitation I said, "It sounds just great! Of course I'll do it." We then discussed some of the details in order for me to come prepared with all the necessary supplies for the art classes. I had a little more than two weeks to prepare myself and fly to L.A. and taxi to San Pedro's harbor. I decided to teach tissue paper collage, a simple and quick method to produce colorful pictures. The supplies are reasonable and easy to distribute to all the passengers that might sign up. I bought enough for one hundred people, but thinking I would only have twenty or thirty students in a class. Everything fell into place like a jigsaw puzzle. I was ready for my departure and was getting excited about the challenge.

The flight to Los Angeles was uneventful and the drive to the harbor was much longer than I had anticipated. The great white ship was very beautiful in the California sunshine on the blue Pacific Ocean. Passengers were supposed to board ship at three p.m. and I was early. Luckily I was allowed on board.

After arriving in my cabin, which was decorated in nice soft colors and had a mirrored wall, I saw a lovely bouquet of pink roses on the dresser. There was a card from Lisa: "Don't unpack, just come as you are to my stateroom, Cabin 226, where a big hug awaits you." Although my hair was a mess, I followed her advice, and found the door to her cabin wide open. Inside her room, larger than mine, were several people with drinks in their hands. She came over immediately, putting her arms around me. "Gang," she announced, "this is our artist in residence, Hilda from Chicago."

I met the ship's photographer, who was married to a singer-dancer. A Latin dance instructor similarly was married to the Tango teacher. There was also the purser, Alfredo, handsome in his white uniform. Lisa said that all the "entertainers," including me, would be introduced at the captain's reception that very night. After the other guests left, I thanked Lisa for providing me with the opportunity to trade art lessons for the cruise. She hugged me, and told me she would see me at second-seating dinner, where the entertainment staff would be dining together.

Back at my cabin, two suitcases were waiting for me, but where was my carry-on bag? I walked down to the purser's desk to inquire, and after Alfredo assured me correctly that it would eventually show up, he fished out several messages for me, including a note from Lisa, a letter from Diana, and another from Paul. The purser recommended that I not trouble myself waiting for the carry-on luggage in the cabin, but instead to "go to the Princess Lounge, have a drink at the bar, and, by the way, since you are entertainment staff, your bar bills are at a steep discount." It made me smile since I did not drink any alcohol. "There will be dance music, and a pretty lady like you will have lots of partners to dance with." I thanked him, but I returned nevertheless to the cabin, where I could run the hot water of the shower to steam out my dress and also read those letters in privacy.

Lisa's note had instructions about my table arrangements. I was to dine with the Italian musicians and the Latin dance duo from Brazil. Furthermore, she said, I should dress informally for tonight's event in the ballroom when the Captain would introduce us all.

There was a knock on the door of the cabin. An officer with a tanned face, dark eyes and hair introduced himself as the ship's doctor, and explained he had been asked to escort me later to the captain's quarters. He took my hand in his and held it much too long. His eyes seemed to burn holes in my body and I felt extremely uncomfortable. He produced a bottle of champagne and went to the dresser for the tray with two glasses. "Doctor, I don't drink," I said. "You must excuse me, I have to change my clothes and freshen up from my long trip. I'll see you at the Captain's quarters as soon as I get ready."

Unceremoniously, he slammed the door shut to the hallway with his foot, grabbed me, and tried to push me onto the bed. With all my might I struggled free from his unwelcome embrace and screamed at him to get out.

"Carissima, I saw you arrive and I think you are so beautiful." He made no move to leave.

"Get out now! I will tell everyone on the ship that you tried to rape me! Never speak to me again!" I was shaking like a leaf and I was furious and scared. He now turned around to leave. I quickly reached for the bottle of wine and threw it at him. It hit his back and fell, shattered, and spilled all over the corridor floor.

By now, my anger turned to tears and I telephoned Lisa. She was equally upset, but assured me that nothing like that would happen again, that she would take it up with the captain. The doctor would certainly get a sharp reprimand and warning. Personally, I thought he should have been summarily fired. I was ready to turn around and go home, but I felt the movement of the motors, and as I looked out the large picture window, I could see the shore disappearing. We were on our way to Mexico.

What would Charley have done to that beast of a doctor? Thinking of Charley made me feel calmer. He always knew what to do and never lost his cool. I could just hear him say: "Calm down my love. Just ignore that man and don't be afraid. The captain has a little kingdom on the ship and he does not want this to get around to passengers or to the press. You will be safe. Go and enjoy yourself."

How I missed Charley! He had been my right arm. My friends believed me to be self-assured and strong, but it was Charley's backing that held me up and enabled me to appear that way. Now I felt so lost without him. The twenty-eight years we were together had been good years. My childish obsession about Paul nearly had ruined our marriage. Were it not for that, my love for Charley would have been even more complete. Charley was such a decent human being, so unconditionally devoted to me, to Diana, and to my parents. He gave me everything I ever wanted. He even spent endless hours in art museums, which, I know, was a sacrifice for him.

I cried, but needed to pull myself together for the mandatory lifeboat drill. I put on my clumsy life-vest, and headed to one of the on-deck assembly areas, which were assigned by cabin number. After listening to instructions, the drill was over and I watched the coastline in the far distance, and the deep ultramarine blue water, which when churned by the ship, boiled and bubbled with foam of pure titanium white. The sea breeze wrought havoc with my expensive hairdo from Chicago.

A woman in her cumbersome life vest stumbled and fell against me. I bumped into the man in front of me, domino-like. There were apologies all around, and we introduced ourselves, joking about our misadventure. Anne Hall, who was first to lose her balance, and her husband, invited me to dine with them. So too did the man into whom I stumbled, Morton a Chicagoan. However, I was committed to eat with the entertainment staff, so we decided to meet at ten p.m. in the ballroom.

Prior to a reception in the Captain's cabin, I had a short conference with Lisa to set the schedule and location for the three classes I would teach each week. My own art classes in Chicago regularly attracted two dozen students, and I was really curious about how many people would attend my classes during the two-week roundtrip voyage between Los Angeles and Acapulco. Lisa said she was certain my classes would be successful.

After what had happened with the doctor, I felt uneasy going to the captain's reception alone. If only I had an escort, I thought. But the captain's quarters teamed with people, and Lisa, wearing a red feather boa around her shoulders, greeted guests as we came in. Next to her stood the captain and the ship's doctor. I swallowed hard, put on my best smile, shook hands with the Captain, who warmly bid me welcome and inquired about my trip to California. After a few more pleasantries, I passed the doctor quickly and made my way toward the crowd at the bar. I felt less shaky with a glass of Perrier with lime in my hand. My simple black cocktail dress appeared to be a perfect choice for this event. Black was the order of the day.

"You are the artist from Chicago—Lisa pointed you out," said a lovely woman. "I'm Martha. I'm in charge of shore excursions. We will see a lot of each other and you can rely on me to answer your questions. We are like a family here and you are a new member of it."

I was appreciative that she had made a point of greeting me, perhaps intuitively understanding that I felt overwhelmed and ill at ease.

At dinner, however, I was on my own. Martha and I were on opposite sides of the huge dining room. The Maitre d' showed me to my table where I found the seven Italian musicians already seated. They jumped up to greet me. All of them were very polite, but they spoke as little English as I spoke Italian. Being with them throughout dinner was a chore that I hoped would become easier after a while. Carlo, on my left, was quite attentive. He told me his instrument was the saxophone. Guiseppe, to my right, was a singer. They seemed to understand, while I struggled to tell them, that I was looking forward to hearing them play in the main lounge.

Lisa, at last, appeared at the table. "Ducks, it is time for the intros in the ballroom," she announced. She looked fabulous in her all-red gown, feather boa and stage make-up. "Did you enjoy your seven dinner partners?" she asked privately. "It is only for the first week. On the return leg, you will get to sit at a different table and meet more of the entertainment staff."

The Grand Ballroom was very beautiful. Its huge stage had a shimmering curtain. The captain and his staff lined up in front of it, every one of them looking splendid.

Lisa instructed me to sit in the first row of seats and be prepared to walk up to the Captain when my name was called. By now, all the passengers were in their seats. The lights dimmed and Lisa, on stage, welcomed everyone. She told a little joke and then had everyone repeat after her. "This is *fantastic.*" That word became her mantra throughout the cruise.

The Captain introduced his staff members then handed the microphone back to Lisa for the introductions of singers, dancers, orchestra conductor, portrait artist, photographer, and then me. It was easier than I had expected. I thought it went well. Then my dinner partners played dance music and the guests danced on stage.

Angelo, the chief engineer, asked me to dance. It was nice. He spoke English well and we had an interesting conversation. He told me of his family. His wife was in Milan, but his three sons were following maritime careers. His eldest was a purser on a ship plying the Mediterranean. The middle son was attending naval academy in Naples. The youngest worked in a shipyard in the summers between high school classes. For the chief engineer, a typical tour of duty lasted six months, but his wife was used to the long separations. He hoped she would be able to join him when the ship went to the Caribbean.

Finally, I returned to my cabin, undressed, brushed my teeth, and took my letters into bed with me. Diana had written that she was chosen as a contestant on two television quiz shows, "Who, What, Where?" and "Jeopardy." She was so excited to tell me that she had won $9,000, a barbecue, sheets, brick wallpaper and other household items. I was so proud of my smart and very attractive daughter. But I was not at all surprised that she did well! She always had!

Paul said he had wanted to meet me in Acapulco and cruise back with me to Los Angeles; however, business precluded him from doing so. Besides, his wife was sick and he could not leave her. Despite myself I was disappointed. He kept making plans and then changing them. Why did I leave myself open to this? Why did I still have feelings for him? My new resolution was to distance myself from him once and for all, and grow up. I would end this obsession, which could only lead to pain and trouble. With that sensible plan, I tore up his letter and I went to sleep.

At my first class the next morning, I found that seventy-eight passengers had signed up. That was an overwhelming number for one teacher, so Rita, a server in the Lido Bar, was assigned as my helper, and she proved quite helpful. I decided to get a clip-on microphone so that everyone in the class could hear me. To my surprise, all went extremely well. It was lots of fun. We distributed a packet of colorful tissue papers, a jar of white glue, a brush, a cup of water, and a canvas board to each student. At the end of the hour, many of them produced very attractive collages. Nobody wanted to leave. They all asked if they could stay longer and return to the next class. I stayed an extra half hour surrounded by my students, who wanted me to see their "masterpieces." Their enthusiasm and interest was most rewarding, and in some cases, so were their collages. I could not wait to tell Lisa.

My lifeboat drill acquaintances came by to remind me of our plans to have lunch together at one o'clock. I decided to stroll around the deck several times in the interim to unwind. Lots of other passengers had the same idea, so the Promenade Deck was lively along the walking path. Elsewhere, other passengers lounged on deck chairs reading, napping or sipping Margaritas. On my third circuit around the deck, Morton from the lifeboat drill intercepted me, and we had a nice conversation. I learned his law practice was on La Salle Street in Chicago and that he had booked the cruise to recuperate from a bitter divorce. He commented on my slight accent, which he assured me he found charming. He said that he realized after the Captain introduced me that a cousin of his owned one of my paintings.

I, in turn, told him that I had been recently widowed and that I felt very uncomfortable being on the ship by myself after having traveled regularly with my husband of twenty-eight years. Work to do on the ship was a life saver for me. I commented that modern-day cruise ships were certainly quite different from the last time I had been at sea, in 1940, chased by Nazi submarines from England to New York. I told him that I had flown to Mexico before for land vacations but never had visited the country by cruise ship. My father had a distant cousin whom we met when we traveled with Diana, who was then a little girl. We made some repeat visits to Mexico City and to the cousin's condo in Acapulco as well. But some of the ports we would be visiting on this cruise—Cabo San Lucas, Mazatlan and Puerto Vallarta—were new to me and I looked forward to seeing them.

Martha subsequently asked me if I would be willing to help her get the passengers to their right buses and serve as an escort. I was delighted with the prospect because this meant that I not only would see the ports, but also would be in good company. I dreaded the idea of having to explore the ports on my own.

There was time in Cabo San Lucas to telephone my daughter, "the Quiz Show Winner" and to hear from her all the details of the show. She said on the final question of Jeopardy, another contestant beat her to the buzzer, or she might have won. How much she was like her father! They both had photographic memories and enjoyed storing in them the bits and facts that we call trivia. Charley was amazingly well informed about geography, while Diana excelled at literature, movies and world history.

I relaxed after that, adapting well to both the onboard and shore routines. I should add that the ship's doctor never bothered me again.

My art classes went so well that we were able to arrange for an exhibit of the students' work. Several VIPs were appointed as judges and different souvenirs from the ship were bestowed as prizes. My students were ecstatic, and the captain congratulated me on conducting such a wonderful program. By then I had many friends, so wherever I walked on the ship, someone greeted me. I no longer felt lonely or strange, and when one was needed, Sherman acted as my escort. I really enjoyed being part of the family of entertainers.

My favorite Mexican port was Puerto Vallarta, where we boarded a small ship that took us to Mismaloya, a nearby village where Ava Gardner and Richard Burton filmed "Night of the Iguana." Gardner may have been Burton's co-star by day, but a spectator, Elizabeth Taylor became his passion by night. It was the start of their great romance. Such glamour seemed incongruous in a place like Mismaloya, where pigs ran down the unpaved street. But there was a fantastic small beach, and farther up the hill, a waterfall.

Seeing Puerto Vallarta as well as La Paz and Mazatlan made me hunger to go home to my studio, where I could paint the Mexican markets, the fishermen, the beaches and the ochre-hued landscapes, as well as the jungles of Puerto Vallarta and the puppeteers on the beach.

The time on the ship also helped me sort out my feelings for Paul. I realized that he was part of the past, and that it was time to look forward and not backwards. Part of my future would be repeated assignments as a guest art lecturer aboard cruise ships.

A year later, Lisa took a job aboard Norwegian Caribbean Line, today known as Norwegian Cruise Line. Because of my record on my first cruise, she arranged for me to guest lecture on all of their ships. On one of those cruises I met Esther the wife of the Vice President of the Cruise Line and we became good friends. They introduced me to Ted Arison, who later became the owner of Carnival Cruise Lines, which today is the giant of the cruise ship industry. I believe meeting Ted and Lin, his wife, proved to be the turning point in my career as an artist.

Norm and Hilda Pierce

Hilda and Norm's Wedding 1970

Norm Pierce

After instructing an art class in the penthouse of our apartment building in Chicago Norm picked me up to go to dinner at a nearby restaurant. Instead of sitting across from me in the booth, he sat by my side, his hand touching my arm. It felt warm and wonderful, but my face blushed so that it embarrassed me. For a long time, we didn't speak.

I thanked him again for chauffeuring both Mutti and me home from our respective flights. I produced a bottle of Tanqueray gin that I had purchased on board ship. Pleased, Norm kissed my cheek. "You are not only beautiful, smart and kind but very thoughtful," he said, moving a little closer to me. "You were only gone for a week but it seemed like a year. I can't tell you how much I looked forward to being with you again. I don't mind confessing that I am happier in your company than with any other woman in my life."

"Oh, you tell that to all the girls," I replied, my blood rushing to my cheeks again.

"I bet you found a lot of admirers on the cruise and never gave me a thought—oops, I shouldn't say that, there is this lovely bottle."

He took my hand and kissed it without releasing it while we gave our order to the server. He also ordered a glass of sweet red Dubonnet wine for me and insisted I taste it. It was nice and made my nose tingle and my knees get weak. Was it the unaccustomed wine or this man sitting so close to me? It was only two weeks ago that we met, and part of that time I had been on the cruise.

When we drove home, Norm asked if he could come up to my apartment for a little while. He needed to talk to me some more. We were still in our coats when he put his arms around me and kissed me passionately. He helped me out of my coat, removed his own, took my hand, looked at me closely, and dumbfounded me by asking: "Hilda, will you marry me?"

I burst out laughing and said, "You must be crazy. From what I've heard, you dated every divorcee and widow up and down Lake Shore Drive for the last ten years, so why me?"

"Because I know a diamond when I find one!"

I was flattered but I said, "I think you are pulling my leg. It's late and you have to work tomorrow and I am still on jet lag. Let's talk again tomorrow."

"I meant every word," he declared, and with a peck on my cheek he left.

Norm had a unique way of pursuing me: he took me out to dinner every night and was helpful to me in every way with my career. Norm loved the Art Fairs that I participated in and, without his assistance, I would have had to give them up. He had excellent taste and was a fine and informed critic of my work. All my friends were happy for me to have a new companion and we were very much in love. Though I still talked to Paul a lot, my feelings for him and my obsession over him had faded.

But there were two important reasons for not marrying Norman until September eleven, 1970. First, from the moment it became clear in which direction our relationship was heading, I resolved that I would not re-marry until at least a year had elapsed since Charley's death. Second, tragically, Mutti died in June 1970, and my grief was too intense to want to mix in festivities. I'll never forget how helpful Norm was to me during that period.

Judge Albert Hallet, whose wife Helen was one of my students, officiated at the private ceremony in which Norm and I were married. A photographer friend and the judge's clerk served as our witnesses. We had no guests. Norm had a high fever and we were to depart on our honeymoon trip to Europe on September twelve, the very next day. Poor Norm didn't recover until our plane landed in Athens, Greece.

For all his worldliness, it was Norm's first time in Europe. An artist friend had told me about Santorini, the island that some believe to be located above the sunken city of Atlantis. We arrived by boat from Crete late at night. The ship could not sail into the harbor, so we were transferred into small boats and rowed to the dock. The sea was pitch black, but there were stars right above us.

On shore, we and our luggage were put on donkeys, which climbed a narrow stairway. The side of the mountain was on our right, a balustrade on our left, and the sea was way below us. Up and up we went with the donkeys relieving themselves in front of me.

"Hilda, where are we going?" Norm asked anxiously. "I have never been on a horse before and I thought that Europe meant London and Paris."

I tried to take his mind off the ordeal. "Honey, the guide says that what looked like stars from our boat really are the lights of Santorini on top of this mountain."

"I am scared I might fall into the water below," he replied. "My animal is tripping and slipping."

I truly felt sorry for my new husband. I didn't know that our adventure meant a midnight ride like this. My friend in Chicago hadn't mentioned that part of Santorini's description.

"Just hold on to the saddle, Norm. You won't fall off. It cannot be much longer. The lights are getting closer to us."

At long last we got to the top of the mountain and our hotel. We were helped off the donkeys and with our luggage. Down below us, our ship was as small as a toy boat.

We had reserved the room on the top floor with the marble bath as per my friend's instructions. The room was small, the windows shuttered, the bathroom all marble indeed, except that there was no water. The maid who had taken us there pointed to a bucket next to the toilet. Totally exhausted, we crept into bed and fell asleep.

When we opened the shutters in the morning, our breath was taken away by the sight of blinding white houses stacked one upon the other, some with cupolas blue or gold. There were stairways everywhere, no trees or plants, just rock. The sea was blue like ink, with a few boats in the distance. An even higher mountain was to our left, with what seemed to be ruins at the top. A painter's dream come true. I didn't know Santorini was a waterless island, that fresh water had to be imported on huge rubber rafts.

We met some fascinating people and had a great time during the few days we spent on this magical Aegean island, which seemed straight out of the writings of Homer.

We later found out that a tourist did have a fatal fall from his donkey into the ocean below only a week before we arrived. Luckily, we didn't have to descend by donkey; we took a taxi down the other side of the mountain. We learned that having different methods for ascent and descent was a way to assure both donkey drivers and taxi drivers to earn their living.

We explored a number of other islands and Norm got to like them, but not as much as I did. When I was at school in Vienna, a lot of emphasis had been placed on Greek mythology, so that added another dimension to my appreciation. I imagined I was cavorting with all the Greek gods and goddesses. And I consulted with the Oracle at Delphi when we went there.

Mutti and I had been to Greece two years previously on our way to Israel. However, Norm and I visited different islands. From Greece, it was on to Italy, Austria, Switzerland, and England. It was the first of many great trips Norm and I took together and, like that Mexico cruise, inspiration for many a landscape I would later paint in my studio.

Norm had been particularly excited to see Vienna, the place of my birth, where I showed him all my old haunts, my schools, our apartment, my parents' antique store, the parks where I had played as a child, the museums where my parents and I had spent so many winter Sundays. He loved the Vienna Woods. We had lunch on the Kahlenberg, where I could point out all the churches and important buildings fronting the winding grey Danube below.

In Austria, they call Jack Frost "Farbenmanderl" (Little Color Man). He had done his work well. The trees and bushes were tinged in glorious colors. Austria looked splendid—much more so than I had remembered it from my early childhood. The streets of Vienna, on the other hand, were not nearly so wide as I had recalled. In fact, the major streets were no wider than the side street where our apartment building was located in Chicago.

Norm and I ended our Vienna Woods lunch with "*Sachertorte mit Schlag*" (chocolate cake with whipped cream), and then found a bench at the edge of the cliffs where, with his arm around me, I recounted the story of the terrible last year of my life under the Nazi regime.

We talked until five, when the church bells summoned us back to our hotel to dress for dinner.

The next morning, Norm and I met with Ilan and Michael, sons of my cousin Fritz and his former wife Trude, whom I loved. Fritz had returned to Israel, but his sons had remained in Austria with their mother. They drove us to what used to be my grandparents' farm house in Lassee. I showed them the house that my grandfather had built about the time of Mutti's birth in 1890. It still was in good condition.

There we rang the bell and an old woman with a babushka came out. I told her who I was, and she said: "I, too, am named Eveline, like your mother."

"Oh, did you go to school with her?" I asked.

"Oh, no, I am your age." We were stunned—and later, on our way home, laughed a lot about my *faux pas*. Eveline allowed us to walk around the yard, to the stables, and into the house. It was nicer than I had remembered it. In my mind's eye I could see my grandmother feeding her chickens. My favorite Uncle Karl lifting me onto his shoulders and taking me for a walk into the stables. My mother sitting on the veranda embroidering a table cloth with cross stitch flowers. But this flashback disappeared in a second or so. After taking our leave, we walked to the nearby war memorial where the names of World War I veterans were listed, hoping to find that of my Uncle Karl's. However, his name had disappeared. The Nazis had eradicated it because "Karl Kohn" was the name of a Jew.

How I wanted to tell my young cousins to leave that country of hatred and tragedy! But one was married to a Viennese girl, a Gentile, and the younger one still was in medical school. Their mother, Trude, and grandmother owned a big apartment building and a boutique in Vienna. They seemed content there. That was difficult for me to understand.

Norm and I next went to London, retracing my odyssey as a young refugee. He especially enjoyed being in London, where he did not face a language barrier. A devotee of William Shakespeare and Arthur Conan Doyle, he felt right at home there. He didn't even mind driving on the left side of the road.

We drove through Copthorne, where I had stayed with Isobel Blaikie and her daughter Muriel, but nothing looked familiar. Nobody could help us find Christmas Lane, so, disappointed, we continued on to Bristol. Though Norm had adapted readily to driving on the left, England's roundabouts posed greater difficulty for him. We arrived at the flat of Brenda Roseveare Wright in Bristol much later than planned. She had helped arrange a party that Norm and I planned to host the next day.

Nevertheless, we received a warm welcome and the party for my beloved English family was successful. They had gathered from all over England. I felt so loved and honored to be among them after so many years. I had seen many of them on other trips, but having them all together was a special treat. Isobel had died years before, but Muriel was there. So were Auntie Marjory, who was widowed by then; lovely Brenda and her husband Phil; and Rob and Paddy Roseveare. Norm was delighted to meet them all and they were equally happy to meet him. I thought of these great people as my wonderful English family.

"I have never met a more wonderful group of people," Norm confided. "Now I can truly understand how fortunate you were to find a home with them when you most needed one. You can be very proud that they, too, consider you part of their family." Norm was truly overcome by the group, all of them so educated and intellectual, with distinguished careers, yet so humble and unaffected. And of course, they were so very English with their elegant speech.

Home once again, we decided to convert Norm's apartment into an office and live in my apartment. We got along beautifully and I learned that I had not only gained a husband, I also had found a public relations director in the bargain who was helpful in obtaining publicity for my art.

Norm Pierce had started his own sound slide film business after twenty-two years in radio and television in Chicago, where his was a household name. He was very inventive, enthusiastic and talented and I admired his passion for music and art. I loved him for his warmth and adoring attitude toward me. We were a team.

Both of us had lots of friends and an active social life. By then, our children were married and had fine careers of their own. My paintings of European, Mexican, and American landscapes, as well as of children, sold well at the prestigious art fairs in Chicago. Since I had filled several sketchbooks on our honeymoon in Europe, I had lots of material to paint.

California

The winters in Chicago were very severe and my hands became swollen and pained, so much so that I couldn't paint. We decided to move to a better climate. We drove to Florida but found that we wouldn't like to stay there year-round. As for snow-birding, we believed that shuttling back and forth from Chicago to Florida would become too strenuous in time.

We explored Tucson, Arizona, even picking out a lot and finding a builder. It was a beautiful spot on the side of the mountains with a fabulous view over the city of Tucson. We looked at it also at night and the lights of the city looked like a jewel box filled with diamonds. After a heavy downpour the next day we returned to our prospective site to meet with an architect. The people who were building a house next to our lot already had dug a foundation. the deep hole was filled to the brim with rainwater. In it, writhing, were a hundred or more rattlesnakes. They had been washed down the mountain. That sight eliminated Tucson for us.

We had acquaintances in Laguna Beach, California, and went to see them. We immediately fell in love with the beauty of that little art colony. A realtor showed us to a very unusual rental house. Unusual—because nobody before could get along with the owner who had a lager house on the same grounds.

It was an estate of great charm. It had a fabulous view of Bluebird Canyon, the Pacific with Catalina Island in the distance, a two-acre garden with fountains, fruit trees, and an abundance of flowers.

We decided to take a chance on living in peace with our neighbor and rented the house. Our landlord was indeed eccentric but we endured him, we so adored the house. His wife and I became friends. My hands became normal in no time and I could paint without pain and be inspired by the wonderful light and scenery of this enchanting place.

On November twenty-five, 1975, a month after we moved to Laguna Beach, we had wonderful news. Our granddaughter Melissa was born in Westport, Conn. She was the most delightful baby. We were jubilant.

California housing prices were escalating at an alarming rate, but our rental house was so exquisite that no other house could compare with it. Nevertheless, we wanted to buy a home. Three years after moving to California, we purchased a big new house in Laguna Niguel, just south of Laguna Beach. We also opened a gallery on Coast Highway, on Gallery Row, to show and sell my work..

Norm had a very difficult time adjusting to the change from Chicago, his birthplace, where he was a well-known personality, to a small village where he had neither work nor any friends. He was the one who had insisted that we move to a climate that would help me be free of pain, but his disposition changed. He became depressed and unhappy.

I hoped that being in the gallery would be good for him. I was convinced that my paintings would sell well. The artists represented in the other galleries were very different, and we really went all out to make the Hilda Pierce Gallery a showplace. Stark white walls, great lighting, light gray carpeting, no clutter, just my colorful paintings, shown like in a museum. This contrasted with other galleries that were dark and filled with hanging pots and lots of plants in a style they called "Laguna charm."

My works were framed and painted with the finest materials in the style that had won prizes in Chicago and which had passed numerous juries, and had also been accepted to be shown at the Art Rental and Sales Gallery of the Art Institute of Chicago. My husband was to man the gallery and I would stay in my studio and paint. He worked there without salary and I gave my paintings to the gallery.

I was used to selling my work as fast as I could paint it, but not in Laguna Beach. We were spectacularly unsuccessful. Our gallery was not what the local clientele liked. My work was slightly abstracted, higher priced than the souvenir type pictures. We did not break even financially.

People from the eastern states did buy an occasional painting. For the locals, we tried a different marketing approach. We hosted dinner parties in the beautiful roof garden restaurant of the hotel across the street from our gallery, the Surf and Sand. Our guests had a wonderful time and when we all came back to the gallery, they were very complimentary but no sales resulted.

My friend Lisa invited Norman and me to cruise on an NCL ship for a second honeymoon. Part of the deal was that I was to again teach painting. This was the cruise on which we met Ted and Lin Arison. He then was in partnership with the Kloster family, owners of Norwegian Caribbean. I became friends with Lin Arison, the vice president, his wife and daughter. The latter two attended my on-board art class.

Subsequently, the Arisons visited our gallery in Laguna Beach and purchased five of my largest paintings. That was very exciting. Gathering up all my courage, I asked Mr. Arison to let me do the art work on his next new ship. By now, he owned Carnival Cruise Lines.

"My dear Hilda, with my purchases I have proven to you that I think you are the best woman artist in the country. I admire your work immensely but for my ships I need artists with a world-wide reputation and name recognition." he replied.

"Well, anyone can buy a Picasso painting, but you could help make me into a Picasso." I countered.

He and his wife laughed and he said to let him think about it. Norm pinched my arm and I understood he meant that I should not pursue the matter further.

The Arisons said they were returning home on their private jet, and I asked if it were big enough to carry the large paintings. Lin Arison smiled. "It is big enough, it is a 727, but we would prefer that you ship them to Florida."

After that, Norm's mood lifted and he was happier and more like himself. He particularly enjoyed a visit from Tom and Minnie Friedman of Austin, Texas, who had gone to high school and to drama school with him. Tom was a psychology professor at the University of Texas in Austin, and also ran a children's summer camp on his ranch up in the Texas hill country.

Their children, like Diana, were already grown: Roger, the eldest, also a psychology professor, was married and had a child in Baltimore. Richard, who went by the nickname of "Kinky," was an aspiring author in New York. Marcie, the youngest, was completing her doctoral studies at UC Berkeley.

Despite his lifting spirits, Norm was not really well. Once he blacked out and at other times he felt numb and walked with a peculiar tilt. By the time the Friedmans returned to Austin and called to thank us for our hospitality, I had taken Norm to Scripps Clinic in La Jolla. After numerous tests, they found that he had a brain tumor that needed surgery. A surgeon to whom people came from all over the world performed the operation. However, when Norm came out of the recovery room, he felt paralyzed from the neck down. The surgeon thought it would get better later on.

I closed the gallery. Diana, Everett and ten-year-old Melissa moved to Newport Beach, California. It was comforting to have them close by. Norm loved Melissa and was a real grandfather to her, and she loved to come and paint with me.

Norm suffered untold agonies during his treatment. Radiation and all kinds of horrible tests made him hallucinate. It was hell on earth. The surgeon kept telling me he would get better, but I could see that there was no hope. If he survived, he would remain totally paralyzed. The Friedmans called us at the hospital every other day, and numerous other friends did what they could to show their concern and to lift our spirits.

I looked at various nursing homes, but found them all too depressing. I decided to bring Norm home and get help for him. However, after forty days in the hospital, he died in March 1985. The surgeon and I were both at his bedside. Although his fingernails were turning blue, Norm died without seeming to have any pain. He just faded away. He did not want to live if he could not be whole. He was sixty-nine years old.

It was heartbreaking and unbelievable. How could fate be so cruel? Norm's son Ken had come to see his father. I had told him Norm's condition was terminal, but Ken, who had talked to the surgeon, thought that I might be exaggerating. Oh, I wish that I had been! We lost Norm. I drove home to my large empty house. I have no recollection how I got there.

Tom and Minnie called and when I gave them the news they cried with me.

Then just two months later, Minnie Friedman died. As they had cried with me when Norm passed away, now I cried with Tom. After a visit with Marcie in Berkeley, Tom came to Laguna Niguel where, having the tragic loss of our spouses in common, we consoled each other. He suggested that I visit him in Texas and see his ranch. I said I would think about it, but at the time I was not ready to go anywhere.

Fantasy

That winter I was invited to Lin Arison's fiftieth birthday party in Miami. I arranged to fly to Miami and, on my return to California, go via Texas in order to be able to accept Tom Friedman's invitation to visit him.

As a surprise for Lin, I asked Ted to send me a photo of her as a child. He found a photograph of her as a charming three-year-old, which I used as the basis for an oil portrait.

Some 200 people from around the world gathered at the Intercontinental Hotel in Miami for three days of festivities as Ted Arison's guests. The first night was a formal dinner in the grand ballroom. In the long corridor leading to it, costumed mimes, in various poses, silently pointed the way. The decorations in the great ballroom were spectacular, in black and silver. Each guest received a lovely gift. After the wonderful dinner, the beginning of "Singing in the Rain" was shown on a large screen. But after a few scenes, Debbie Reynolds and Donald O'Connor in person came out singing and dancing. And then, they proceeded to roast Lin with some very funny stories. It was an evening to remember.

The next day, we were taken to the harbor where we boarded the M.S. *Celebration*, the first of eight very large sister cruise ships. On this one, Bjorn Winblad, the famous Danish artist, had done all the paintings in the public rooms. The ship was very beautiful and I was introduced to the architect Joe Farcus, who had designed not only the signature ship's funnel but also the interiors of the vessel. After luncheon, we toured the entire ship.

A smaller group was invited to the Arisons' apartment in Miami Beach for a Chinese dinner that evening. Their German Expressionist art collection was most impressive. My large triptych of Mykonos took over a large wall in their bedroom.

My dinner partner was Arthur Hailey, author of *Hotel* and many other books. Yacov Agam, the Israeli artist, as well as the governor-general of the Bahamas and his wife also were at that table. Later Bjorn Winblad came over to compliment me on my work. Coming from an artist of his stature, the compliment was truly an honor.

Lin brought in my wrapped painting, opened it, and shrieked with delight. She hung it on the wall of the dining room, while all the guests applauded. I was flattered and delighted.

Ted Arison took me aside and asked me to meet him at his headquarters at ten the following morning. He said he wanted to discuss my being commissioned to do all the art work for the next Carnival ship, the M.S. *Fantasy.*

"By the way, did Lin tell you that Bjorn Winblad told her that he liked your paintings better than any other in our entire collection?" Ted told me. I was overjoyed and thanked him profusely.

The exciting appointment the next day meant postponing my plans to visit Tom Friedman, Norm's best friend, in Texas, en route to California.When I telephoned and I explained the reason, he expressed delight, and said he couldn't wait to hear more when I arrived.

At the Carnival Cruise Line offices, I was ushered into a room, where eight men were already sitting around a conference table. Ted was seated at the head. I was totally intimidated; I could feel my heart pounding in my mouth.

Before the meeting I had a forty-five minute interview with the interior architect-designer Joe Farcus. I had brought a portfolio of my work and he seemed very impressed and complimentary.

After the introductions in the board room, I was asked to do twelve hundred lithographs for the staterooms of the future cruise ship the M.S.*Fantasy* that was being built in Helsinki, Finland. Because I had no experience with lithography, I suggested monoprints, a method of producing single original images. I had done monoprints at college, one per-day. We agreed to the commission of all twelve-hundred large monoprints. (Monoprints or single-image prints are individual works of art. Each one is painted on a slick surface, in my case a sheet of acrylic, and then has a paper put on top of the wet printer's ink painting and is put through the electric press. Only one image is taken off the slick surface, which is called the plate. The large print is then put in a drying rack) It was an enormous undertaking.

At that point, in the Carnival conference room, I did not realize what such a quantity meant, nor did I take into consideration the large size required. The execution of such a huge amount of originals was well beyond my experience.

"What about the large murals in the sixteen elevator lobbies?" I asked.

Joe Farcus, said the commission for those had not been given out yet. These were, of course, seen by hundreds of passengers.

"Oh, that is what I most want to do. Oil paintings are my favorite and most successful work. It was my hope to get that order and for that purpose, I brought along sketches and photos of my paintings here in my portfolio. Mr. Farcus has seen them and he can tell you about my work."

After some discussion among the gentlemen, I was given the job. My head was spinning and I was happy, but speechless. When Ted asked me about my fees, I told him I would leave it up to him. I would accept what the other artists were paid since the order was the same size for the same-size ship. I did not have the faintest idea what I should charge.

A price was established. I agreed to it, although I had absolutely no inkling what kind of time, effort, and cost of supplies would be required for such an immense number of paintings. I did not know where I could do the work, which necessitated an electric press of a huge size. The oils I could do in my garage. Each of the sixteen murals was to be about twelve feet wide and six feet high, painted in oil on linen canvas.

We shook hands all around and I signed the contract. What a plum of a dream job! I had to pinch myself in order to realize that I was awake, and really had a contract of such magnitude in my briefcase. If only Norm were alive to share this triumph with me. Without his help and advice, I could never have come to that point in my career.

Telling Diana about it on the phone, the enthusiasm and pleasure she expressed made me feel great.

"Mother, I do hope you will have a great time in Austin with Norm's old friend," she said. "I am glad you listened to me when I urged you to accept his invitation to see his ranch. After all, you have never been to Texas, and now it will give you an opportunity to calm down after Miami."

"Don't I always listen to my brilliant daughter?" I replied.

Texas

Tom took me to the Hyatt Regency Hotel in Austin after he had told me that Marcie and a girlfriend had been staying at his house and he did not feel it was in shape to receive a visitor. Next, we drove to Tom's house to meet Marcie. I was looking forward to getting to know her over dinner. However, she was not friendly, and Tom and I ended up going to the restaurant alone. He suggested that instead of staying in Austin, we go instead to his Hill Country Ranch where his son, Kinky, and a friend were staying. The next morning we drove to the ranch. Kinky was nice, and I enjoyed meeting him and his friend.

The ranch was lovely, set in a very green meadow surrounded by hills and a green cedar forest. Near the lodge were the cabins and other ranch buildings of the camp. A bubbling creek running down an embankment had been dammed off, creating the old swimming hole. Large gray deer, twenty horses and Tom's dog, Sam, roamed freely in the open spaces. Bluebonnets, the Texas state flower, made cool pools of shade among the cedars.

It was funny that Tom had named his dog "Sam" because in actuality "Sam" was Tom's real name. He had played the part of Tom Sawyer in a school play and the nickname "Tom" stuck.

The nearest town to Tom's ranch was Kerrville, twenty-one miles away, where Tom belonged to the country club. His closest neighbor, who had built a fabulous mansion and guesthouses, lived six miles away.

At night, armadillos came out. I had never seen these prehistoric, armored animals in the wild. And the stars at night do shine extra bright deep in the heart of Texas.

Tom was a great host. He gave a little party for me at the nice country club in Kerrville. I enjoyed his friends, who were all very warm and friendly. It was a lovely visit and I really enjoyed myself, but I was anxious to get home and start working on my great, challenging commission.

Tom tried to talk me into staying a little longer and I must admit I was tempted. I particularly enjoyed his stories about the times when he, Minnie and Norm all were trying to become actors. He also told me about his own experiences as a B twenty-four navigator during the war on bombing runs over Germany. He had flown an amazing thirty-five missions and was awarded the Distinguished Flying Cross.

Being with him was very pleasant and comfortable. He pleaded with me to return in the summer with my little granddaughter Melissa, while his camp was in session. When he brought me to the airport in San Antonio, he embraced me at the gate, kissed me, and seemed reluctant to let me go. I was startled but not displeased.

The next day, back at my home, a huge bouquet of red long-stemmed roses arrived. Tom followed up with a telephone call and we chatted a long while. As there were three other couples living in Southern California who had been in drama classes with Norm, Tom and Minnie, I decided to give a dinner party for them and invite Tom to join us. One of the men had served as the "Voice of America" in Rome, where he and his wife had lived for many years. Norm and I had visited them in Rome. Another couple owned summer stock theater companies in the Catskills. I don't recall what the third couple did. Everyone had a good time, with one of the ladies even bringing out their high school yearbook. Looking at Norm's picture reminded us all what a tragedy his premature death had been.

Already at work on my monoprints in the Los Angeles studio of the well-known printer, my routine was to stay at the New Otani Hotel and to walk to the studio located on the edge of the Little Tokyo neighborhood. I took the train home on weekends.

Making those large prints was fun. The assistants mixed the lithographic inks for me, carried the large plates to the electric press, then lifted off the print and showed me the result of my painting.

Tom visited me at the print shop and said he was overwhelmed by the amount of skill and labor that was involved. Many well known artists who also used this workshop would occasionally stop in to speak with Tobey the master printer, and looked at my work. From them I learned the names of some wonderful suppliers. I then used them as I worked on the commission. My materials came from east and west, and everything fell into place like a huge jigsaw puzzle. Every day Tom called me and we planned a vacation trip to the Canadian Rockies. At the same time, I spoke to Paul weekly, but I had gotten over my obsession for him some time ago. He took an interest in my career, even helping me to get a gallery connection in New York City. His old friend from Vienna days owned the Selected Artists Gallery on Madison Avenue and showed my work.

After three and a half months at the printer's workshop, I actually had painted fifteen hundred monoprints, each one different. My back was breaking. I needed a vacation before tackling the oil paintings.

We flew to Vancouver, Canada, the staging point for our trip to the Rockies, Lake Louise, glaciers, Banff and some marvelous hotels. Tom and I really enjoyed being together and reveled in scenery that was unforgettable.

We decided to get married after I completed the Carnival commission. During the camp season, I would live with Tom at his ranch in Texas, whereas the rest of the year he would live with me in Laguna Niguel.

We were married in January 1988 and went to Hawaii for our honeymoon. Tom's good friends stayed in a nearby hotel and we had a wonderful time. Tom's son, Roger, from Baltimore arranged to have a basket of fruit and champagne sent to us, along with a note wishing us well. He included in it an admonishment to his father not to forget Minnie, his late wife. I was nonplussed by the note.

After our honeymoon, Tom flew to Texas to get the ranch ready for the camp season and I went to Laguna Niguel, to pack and to pick up Melissa. Readying the camp was a labor-intensive process. The grounds had to be mowed, cabins repaired from winter damage, supplies ordered and put away, and the horses brought back from their winter quarters and groomed properly. The process usually took three weeks, and it was decidedly a family affair.

Marcie and the counselors arrived for orientation a week before the campers arrived. Roger and his wife, who were both psychologists, worked at the camp. They brought their three-year-old daughter with them. Kinky, meanwhile, was living in a little old green trailer on the ranch with his many cats.

I had purchased a gorgeous toy cat at FAO Schwartz for Tom's little granddaughter since Tom said that she liked Kinky's cats

It was difficult for me to leave home and my studio with all the empty canvases to be painted, but Tom wanted me with him, and I, too, wanted to be with my new husband, and to help however I could in this new to me intriguing family business.

Melissa was nervous and excited anticipating her first camp experience. We flew to San Antonio to meet the campers who were arriving from all over the country as well as Europe and Israel. I gathered all the arriving children at the airport, took them to the assembly point and waited for the buses that would take them and their mountains of duffle bags to the ranch, about an hour's drive away.

Many of the children knew each other from previous years, and were hugging, laughing and singing.

"Grandma, I don't know anybody," Melissa whispered in my ear, with tears in her eyes.

"Just wait an hour or so and that will change," I replied, putting my arms around her.

The buses were delayed in Austin, where they picked up other campers. It was extremely difficult keeping that large group of children together and not running around the airport. The airport people told us our group was too noisy, and that we needed to move outdoors with all our luggage. I began to feel very anxious, and was upset that Tom had given me this responsibility without proper help or warning. We waited several hours. The bus ride was long and tiring. When we finally arrived at camp, a counselor instead of Tom was there to greet us. The counselor explained that Tom was extremely busy but would meet me at the lodge, where we would be staying.

The counselors separated the campers into groups and took them to their respective cabins. They also sorted out the voluminous mountain of luggage. Melissa was assigned to a cabin with eight other girls her age. I waved to her as she reluctantly followed the group.

When I got to the lodge, I found Roger, his wife and daughter at a picnic table outside, under a large tree, having lunch. We shook hands and I pulled out the toy cat, which was life-size and handed it to the little girl. Her mother grabbed the toy, said the child was severely allergic to stuffed toys. I felt very sorry about that.

Roger said: "I am very happy for you and my father, but my mother's spirit is all over this ranch and you have no place here."

My shock and surprise sent a pounding pain to my temples, as Tom walked up, put his arms around me, kissed me and smiled. "I see you have met some more of my family. We can all have lunch together now. Let's go to the dining hall in half an hour and see the campers have their lunch also." He kept talking about who had come already, and who still was expected on the next two busloads. The bookkeeper, nurse, cooks, wranglers, dishwashers, Marcie and the counselors all had come much earlier.

Getting the camp off to a good start was a huge undertaking, I could see. Minnie had managed the camp before, while Tom was teaching at the university. Now that he had retired from U.T., the entire job was on his shoulders except for the recruitment of new campers, which was in part taken up by Marcie. She had terminated her doctoral studies at UC Berkeley for reasons she did not disclose to me.

We all walked across the corral to the dining hall. There was Melissa and she introduced me to her new best friend Hilary. They were giggling and talking and I was so happy for Melissa. Next we encountered Marcie. She was civil to me, and all the campers seemed to adore her. They jumped up and hugged and kissed her.

Tom took me into the kitchen to introduce me to the staff. The cook had been with the ranch for fifteen years or more. Outside the temperature was at least ninety-five degrees, and how much hotter it was in the kitchen, who knew? It had only two ceiling fans. Nevertheless, the cook seemed inspired. The food was great!

The camp had one-hundred-fifty boys and girls, ranging in age from five to fifteen. They all had changed into their white camp shirts and shorts, and looked clean, spiffy and very happy. The campers of each cabin had their own table in the dining hall, with two counselors assigned to them.

As Roger and his family already had eaten, they left. Marcie ate with the campers. Tom and I sat by ourselves. It was amazing to me how he was able to call all the campers by name. Most of them were returnees, whose parents had been campers in the previous generation. Norm's son Ken also had been a camper and counselor there. Tom was so happy to see them all, I could not spoil his day by telling him about the strange and hurtful welcome Roger had given me.

I found the living conditions in the lodge extremely difficult to adjust to. Our bedroom also was Tom's office and people walked in day and night to talk to him, even if we were already in bed. There was only one shabby bathroom. The living room also housed the gun cabinet. All the counselors had a key for it. They came in and out of the living room whenever they needed to bring the guns to the gun club. This was Texas. All children were taught to shoot guns.

Sam, the large, untrained dog, ate his wet knucklebone that Tom cooked for him daily, on top of the bedspread on our bed.

Marcie had the other bedroom next to ours. The tiny kitchen had a litter box for Kinky's cats next to the table where we had breakfast. The drawers in the bedroom chest had mouse droppings in them. I kept my clothes in my suitcases. The only new and nice building on the ranch was the newly built garage.

A very nice woman came to clean the lodge and I had a good talk with her. We set to work to clean things up as best as was possible and rearranged the furniture. I saw we needed a new mattress, bed linens, towels and some kind of acid to get rid of mold in the shower and new rubber mats to cover the broken tile floor.

The next morning I asked Tom to take me into Kerrville to shop. He bought everything I asked for. Somehow I had to stick it out this first summer. I suggested that we remodel the garage into a nice little apartment for us. We gave the resident carpenter the job to do it. I asked for a large picture window, a nice bathroom and a wall-type kitchen, my gift to the ranch. As the new "annex" shaped up, I realized that the next summer would be better. The only good feature, in the meantime, was that the lodge was air-conditioned.

I taught art classes for the campers in the one-hundred-degree heat of the art shack. None of the children seemed to mind the heat. I, on the other hand, kept thinking about my beautiful house in Laguna's cool summer, which was waiting for us, vacant. I longed to be back there instead of at the ranch where horses roamed freely on the grounds, leaving deposits on my doorstep and where insects of all shapes, colors and sizes abounded. There were walking sticks—ten-inch long bugs with twelve legs—that hung from the trees and plopped down onto the ground in front of you, ants, tiny and huge in many different colors, fleas on the dog and everywhere else.

Tom teased me that my idea of camping was to sit in the lobby of the Ritz Carlton Hotel in Laguna!

The children were extremely happy at the camp. The activities, swimming, horseback riding, hiking, nature studies, arts and crafts, archery, shooting range, singing, drama, tennis, ball games, baseball, and soccer were all well run and highly professionally managed. Tom took pride in the fact that it was not a competitive camp. Children were taught to compete not with each other but with themselves. After all, this was a camp run by three psychology professors.

My husband spent most of his time with Marcie and in meetings with staff members. After learning that a considerable amount of groceries was missing, I found out that they were put in a freezer locker in Kerrville by the cook. I supervised the kitchen and saved hundreds of dollars by checking receipts and keeping inventory of the steaks, roasts, and turkeys to prevent further pilfering.

Kinky was always friendly and nice to me. His first mystery novel I think it was "Musical Chairs," had just been published and he was writing a second one. He was typing in the living room of the lodge. Sometimes he invited me to his dilapidated trailer for tea and we talked about his book or his girlfriends. In his second book he wrote about the Nazi era and I was able to give him some information. Several times he played his guitar and sang for the campers at the evening entertainment time on the tennis courts. The kids loved it.

For the children, the camp was a fine experience. Melissa was extremely happy there. She could hardly wait for the next year. I loved being with the children and seeing them enjoy their activities. However, the climate—neither the hot weather, nor the chill from two of Tom's children—was for me.

Tom was unwilling to tell them that such behavior was unacceptable.

"Hilda, dearest, give them a little more time," he counseled. "They cannot help but fall in love with you once they get to know you. Please wait a while longer. You will see it will not remain a problem."

He refused to talk to them about it, and at every subsequent occasion when we were together as a family, I felt most uncomfortable.

I worked from morning till night doing the layout for the camp's yearbook, teaching arts and crafts and supervising in the boiling hot kitchen. I ate lunches and dinners at different camp tables and helped prepare for the camp play.

Sometimes, after dinner, Tom and I would take a breather on the lawn in front of the lodge. I began to think that Tom enjoyed this exaggerated sense of loyalty that Roger and Marcie displayed to their late mother, a sweet woman with whose memory I had no desire to compete.

In the limited time that Tom spent with me, he was tender and loving, but we really did not communicate openly with each other any more. He worked harder than a man of seventy should. I worried he might have a heart attack from the strain and the heat. I could hardly wait for the end of the camp season. It had been a long hot and difficult summer for me. I had never felt that much alone and friendless. There was no-one I could communicate with. My husband was very busy and tired when we finally were alone together. After all the campers had left the camp had to be prepared for winter. It just seemed an endless workload.

Finally back in Laguna Niguel, I got busy painting the large mural size paintings on the back wall of my garage. There was very good light and I enjoyed working with the garage door open. The house was on a private street in a gated community and we knew all our neighbors. Every now and then one of them would peek in, compliment me and chat for a minute or so. I was pleased with my work and painting on the large canvases was more fun than I ever had before.

Tom kept busy with camp business in the office we had made from one of the downstairs bedrooms facing the golf course. He played tennis almost daily and telephoned his three children every evening. Marcie had accepted a job in Washington D.C. and decided against taking over the ranch camp, which Tom had told me was the plan.

Her decision meant Tom would have to return to the camp the following summer. "Only one more year," Tom consoled me.

By the time the next camp season started again, I had completed all sixteen large murals. The thirty oil paintings for the suites on the ship I painted in my studio in the house. That was next to Tom's office and he watched me paint whenever he looked up from his paper work.

My friends entertained a lot and I reciprocated with dinner parties after working for eight to ten hours each day. I wanted Tom to be happy.

The M.S. *Fantasy* was almost completed when we were invited to come to Helsinki for the christening of the ship by the wife of Finland's president. They also needed me to supervise the installation of my paintings.

On our way to Finland, we stopped off in Copenhagen to see Aspee, with whom my first husband Charley and I had adventures in India back in 1962. Since that time, I had served as an art lecturer on several tours that their H.A.T. tour company ran in Europe. He and Grethe, his Danish wife, had become collectors of my paintings, and I was extremely fond of Aspee's new spouse. They asked me to be godmother to their son, Alistair. Three days in Copenhagen with them were most enjoyable and interesting for Tom and me.

In Helsinki, the ship was still under construction and hard hats were required to go aboard. The bulkheads had niches cut into them, where my murals were installed, as if in a shadow box. Lit from above, the murals were washed by light, setting them off to their best advantage. It was a thrill for me to see them. The lobbies were gorgeous.

We met many fascinating people and were dined and wined, and enjoyed several opportunities to tour Helsinki and environs.

Months later when the *Fantasy* arrived in Miami, Tom and I were guests of honor on the inaugural cruise. The owners of the Line made me feel like queen for a day, each day of the seven-day cruise.

Ted Arison kept telling me that the *Fantasy* was the "Hilda Pierce floating museum" with my 1,246 original works of art on board. He also told me that the next sister ship to the *Fantasy* was already on the drawing boards. The commission to do the art work for it was mine if I wanted it. That was indeed great news and I accepted with thanks.

As the shipyard in Helsinki was just beginning to build the sister ship, I would have some time for rest and relaxation before I would again have to devote virtually all my waking hours to such a project.

We decided to book a cruise to South America as neither of us had been there. Mardi Gras in Rio de Janeiro, along with stops in Buenos Aires and Montevideo sounded great.

Our plane landed in Rio en route to Buenos Aires. Seeing that beautiful city from the air and later from the ship took our breath away, it was so beautiful. We had a few days to enjoy Argentina's capital before boarding the cruise ship and sailing up the Rio Plata to nearby Montevideo. Mutti's brother Rudi had lived there before we brought him to Chicago. The Rio Plata's water stayed brown during much of the voyage.

From the Uruguayan capital, the ship went to Rio de Janeiro next, in time for us to attend Carnival. However beautiful Rio may be from the air, on the ground the city is crime-ridden and dangerous. Skyscrapers had graffiti painted up to their fifth floors. Tour guides served as our security guards making the experience of watching the parade nerve-wracking. Under such circumstances—with the guards feeling compelled to even accompany us to the bathrooms—we did not enjoy the parade. It seemed to drag on for far too long. Next, our trip by cable car up Sugarloaf Mountain was quite scary. High winds buffeted the gondola so that it swayed a lot. I was truly frightened.

My unhappy memories of the Texas Hill Country Camp affected Tom's and my marriage. I had decided that I would not return to the ranch for more than a few days the next summer. All the while hoping that Tom would keep his word and retire. When Tom returned to Texas for the following camp season, I accepted an invitation to exhibit at the outdoor art show in Laguna Beach. I needed a reason for not accompanying him to camp. Tom was very upset.

We came to a parting of the ways in 1991 after a three-year marriage. I felt sad, but also deeply relieved. The divorce was uncomplicated, as we had never co-mingled our assets. It was over and done with quickly. Despite that, I cried a lot and felt lonely and betrayed. Had it not been for irreconcilable differences-not between Tom and me, but between his children and me. We might have made it a lasting loving marriage. Geography was also a problem .As I felt lonely in Texas, I believe Tom felt that way in California.

I was so grateful that Diana, Everett and Melissa lived nearby and that I had the second commission for the ship that Carnival Cruise Line was to name the MS *Imagination.*

There was one last suggestion that Tom made to me before we parted; he said that I ought to write a book about my life. I brushed off the idea at the time, but it stayed with me.

Rancho La Puerta

I needed to do some preparations in 1991 for the twenty-fifth annual Laguna Beach Art Fair, where I had been invited as a special guest artist. Luckily, I had a number of paintings in my inventory. A fellow artist built a booth for me on the outdoor fairgrounds, and a neighbor agreed to manage the booth during my absences. I kept busy, but I still felt sad. Nevertheless, working at the Art Fair, selling paintings, making friends, kept me from feeling too lonely.

I decided to book a week at Rancho La Puerta, the wonderful Spa founded in 1940 by Edmond Szekely, a philosophy professor from Romania, and his wife, Deborah. It featured healthy fruits and vegetables grown right on the ranch in Tecate, Mexico. There were exercise classes, evening lectures and discussions. Some well-known celebrities along with professional men and women, mostly women, came to improve both their health and their minds.

The climate in the high desert is sunny and mild the year around. Originally, accommodations were spartan, when I first heard about the place, very inexpensive, about thirty-nine dollars per week. But that was perhaps forty years ago. Fame and inflation had boosted the price to twenty-five-hundred or more per week, but I felt the expense was warranted because Rancho La Puerta would provide an opportunity to recharge my emotional and artistic batteries. My daughter Diana agreed, encouraging me to go.

A friend drove me to Lindbergh Field, San Diego's airport, where a big bus from Rancho La Puerta had been sent to pick up arriving passengers. There were about twenty-five people already on the bus, most of them slim and young women. There were only four or five men in the group.

We drove for an hour through ochre-colored hills strewn with boulders. At times the landscape changed to green meadows and horse farms. The Mexican border crossing at Tecate is only forty miles east of San Diego. Our passports were examined and we were able to cross over. It was instant Mexico. A nice little plaza with a church and bandstand. Then we drove along the main street with poor and shabby houses and shops.

My fellow bus passengers and I were shocked. Was this the place where Rancho La Puerta was located? Then, only ten minutes later, we were at a beautiful wrought iron gate that slowly swung in and paradise opened up. There were huge tropical trees, shimmering fountains, flowers, cacti and garden paths leading to individual little villas and *Casitas*. You could not help but be amazed and thrilled and glad to have come.

Meals were served in a large, beautiful dining hall, where you were seated with different people at every meal, all of them friendly and interesting. At a table for eight, I made friends with seven young wonderful women. We went on hikes together, to gym classes, sunned ourselves after chatting in the pool and met again at the various lectures and evening programs. It was a delight.

The days just flew by. The last evening, I met a woman who was also an artist. We talked about our work and learning that she lived in the San Diego area, I invited her to drive up the coast and see my studio residence, where I had a number of murals completed for the M.S. *Imagination*.

My bus back to San Diego was leaving at noon Saturday and I delivered my luggage to the bus half an hour before departure. But I felt hungry, so I dashed to the dining hall for something to eat. On the steps was my new acquaintance from the night before and a very tall, nice-looking man in blue jeans and a cowboy hat.

"Hilda, this is my friend Herman. I told him about you last night." she said.

He asked me to join them for lunch but I demurred, since I was in a great hurry to catch my bus. They both insisted, so I sat down with them. Herman mentioned that he knew a lot of single men at John Wayne Airport in Orange County, where he had his office. His friend had told him that I was newly single. He suggested that he could introduce me to some of his unmarried male friends, saying I seemed too nice to be alone.

What a lovely and kind gesture. I gave him my business card, invited them both to be sure to visit me in Laguna Niguel, and then ran for my bus.

Hilda and Herman

Hilda with Noah and Max

Orange County, CA.

A few days later, Herman telephoned and asked me to have dinner with him. He felt we should get to know each other before he could find the right person to introduce me to. He said my house in Laguna Niguel was between his home in Newport Beach and his friend's house in San Diego. I accepted his invitation, and, at his request, suggested a restaurant. On an occasional basis, I had been dating a widely traveled man, who was a music and art lover. He lived out of town. No matter what restaurant I suggested—at his request—he would later criticize it for one fault or another. On the other hand, when Herman and I went to Cannons, overlooking Dana Point Harbor at sunset, Herman exclaimed: "What a great choice! What a fabulous view!" We had a lovely dinner and laughed a lot. When he took me home, he asked if he might take me out again the following weekend. I accepted.

Tall and heavyset, he carried his weight well. He was a former college football player, had a full head of white hair, a handsome face, an easy smile, and blue-green eyes with a twinkle in them. I felt at home and at ease with him. Herman had been widowed after a forty-one-year marriage. The artist, whom I had met on the ranch, and Herman had been in a relationship for three years.

Herman did not mention any of the men he knew, who he thought might be interesting to me. I didn't ask, but wondered about this.

Living alone in my large house was not pleasant. In the evenings I never ventured out alone. Although I had no intention of marrying a fourth time, I missed being around men and hated to be sentenced to the exclusive company of women. An interesting, pleasant male companion would have been most welcome to me.

We had a third dinner date the following week, and the scenario was exactly the same. Herman was charming, very complimentary, very interested in my work and background. Two hours at the restaurant seemed short. He drove me home and as he was about to take his leave, to visit his girlfriend again for the weekend, I felt it was time to clear up the situation.

As I walked him to the door, I said: "Herman, it was really nice getting to know you and going out to dinner with you. But since you did not find anyone to meet me, as you had said you would, and you are committed to another woman, I must tell you ; I was an only child and not used to sharing, particularly not a man. Please accept my thanks but don't call me anymore." I could see that he felt hurt.

"If I were not committed, would you be interested in going out with me?" he asked, taking my hand. Without hesitation I replied, "Yes, I would be."

I really liked him a lot, his easy-going temperament, his gentle manner, his positive attitude. He kissed me gently and hugged me. It felt cozy and warm. "I'll call you tomorrow," he said, as he left.

When next he phoned, he said: "I am not committed anymore." He asked if we could meet the next day in Heisler Park, the breathtaking viewpoint of Laguna Beach.

"I'll look forward to it." was my immediate response.

We met and walked along the cliff overlooking the beach. The calm waves with curling white foam were dissolving slowly as they found the sand. He held my hand and I felt safe, cared for and at home. We found a bench in a lovely spot and sat down.

I asked him to tell me about his life, having told him so much about mine, during those three lovely dinners.

"My life story is neither as dramatic nor as fascinating as yours," he said. "If you insist, here it is: Like you, I was an only child. Though I was born in Chicago, I grew up in Arcola,a very small town in southern Illinois. There, my father was a broom-corn dealer. Did you know that brooms are made of broom-corn? I was very good at football and basketball, probably because of my height. I lettered in football at college.

"Before I graduated, I was drafted into the army and sent to Camp Grant in Wisconsin. Just after the Battle of the Bulge, my field artillery battalion arrived in Koblenz, Germany. By that time, I had transferred into the medics. Medics do not bear arms. I wanted to save lives, not have to kill anyone.

"Koblenz, in Germany's wine-growing region, was a city in ruins. It had been heavily bombed. It needed to be cleaned up and have order restored. Military security had to be put in place. Our battalion, the 209th field artillery, was converted into occupation forces.

"In order to prevent disease from spreading, camps had to be kept very clean and neat. The D.P.'s (Displaced Persons) did not always cooperate, but we were able to rectify that situation simply by telling them they could follow our rules, or be transferred to the Russians, who were encamped on the other side of the Rhine. Since they feared the Russians more than death, it solved our problem.

"After the formal surrender of the Germans, our battalion was shipped back to the United States for regrouping and deployment to the war in the Pacific theater. Everyone expected that we would have to fight our way through Japan. In the meantime, we were given sixty days home leave, which certainly restored our physical and emotional energy. In August, we were sent to a port of embarkation and had been issued our uniforms and equipment, when we heard the news that the atomic bomb had been dropped on Japan. Not long after that, Japan surrendered. The war was over.

"Our orders were changed. We were just waiting to be sent for discharge and home. I served three years in the army. I could have been deferred from military service because my widowed mother was very ill while I was in college. But, both mother and I felt that this was a just war and I had to do my part in it.

"Shortly after I got home, I met Marilyn, a friend of my cousin Rhoda's. I helped my ailing mother run the broom corn business since my father had died. She had been ill for some time but refused to see doctors. I insisted on taking her to Chicago and she was diagnosed with a fatal kidney disease. She was only forty-eight years old when she passed away. It was a terrible blow to me. I realized how she must have suffered, with me in Europe, and being in constant pain, and running a business alone in that small town while her family was in Chicago.

"Marilyn and I were married and I sold the business and opened a Cadillac and Oldsmobile agency in Mattoon, Illinois, with Marilyn's brother, Sidney, as a partner. Our wonderful daughter Marsha was born in November 1954. All went well until Marilyn was diagnosed with cancer. She underwent several operations and we decided I should sell the business so we could move to California.

"Through some fortuitous circumstances, I founded Pan Western Ltd, an aviation business at the Orange County Airport. It was close to where we had an apartment. Marilyn helped in my business, but eventually her cancer metastasized and she required several more operations. By that time, Marsha was in college. She had grown into a beautiful young and gifted woman. Marilyn was able to help arrange Marsha's wedding to Roger "Rocky'" but, sadly, she did not live long enough to meet our grandson, Max."

Herman filled me in on other details of his life. Then, after completing his story, he gave a little sigh of relief and asked if he could kiss me.

We went from that bench to Las Brisas for a drink, where I found that Herman, like me, did not drink alcohol, nor did he smoke. That endeared him to me even more. I had great respect for his independence. We sat on the terrace of that charming restaurant and talked some more. Then he asked me to dinner, and afterwards we ended up in a movie. He could not let me go and I felt the same way.

My granddaughter Melissa was at college in Colorado Springs. Circumstances prevented Diana and Everett from attending Parents' Day there, so I offered to represent them. Herman asked if he could take me to "his" airport. We stopped by the home of Diana and Everett to pick up some things for Melissa, so I had the opportunity to introduce them. We could stay only a few minutes but their meeting went very well.

The flight to Colorado Springs was quite difficult. Just before landing, the pilot announced that the landing gear was not going down and that we would have to make a belly landing. He urged us to look around and memorize the number of rows of seats between us and the emergency exits in front and in back of us. I looked out the window and saw ambulances. Foam was being spread on the landing strip. There were men running about.

I realized that if the landing was not done properly, it could mean the end of our lives. I felt amazingly calm, and thought about how much Herman might miss me. We were told to put our heads in our laps, and then, after landing, to proceed directly to the emergency exits, taking nothing with us. The landing was hard and I could hear some women crying. But we were safe and allowed to deplane normally, thanks to a wonderfully skilled pilot.

When I called home, Diana and Everett certainly were relieved that all came to a happy ending. The airline was called Morris Air, and was never heard from again—at least not by me. Diana also told me during that conversation. "Mother, I am so glad you met Herman. He is a keeper. He is just like Daddy was." She was so right. That was why I felt so comfortable and relaxed with him. We reacted to each other the way Charley and I did.

The festivities and visit at Colorado College were great fun for me. Melissa was happy to have me there. In her dorm room, she proudly showed me the view of Pike's Peak, the mountain that inspired Katharine Lee Bates to compose "America the Beautiful" in 1893.

As I had promised, I telephoned Herman, who was shocked to hear the story of the hard landing earlier that day. There had been no mention of it in the California news media. Of course, he was waiting for me on my return to John Wayne Airport, where he maintained his office. We went to have a quick supper at the Pleasant Peasant restaurant, and Herman could not stop telling me how happy he was to have me back safely.

The following week, there was a big party in one of his hangars where he introduced me to his partners and to the airport officials. I could see how respected he was by everyone and I felt proud to be his friend.

Meanwhile, my work for Carnival Cruise Lines was going well. My abstract murals were fun to paint. For the *Imagination,* my commission was for the large murals only, none for the staterooms. That meant less work and more time to enjoy it. I loved covering those gorgeous large stretched canvasses with my shapes and colors, using my whole body as if I were dancing.

A young art student from the local college helped me with mixing paints; hanging the large paintings on the wall; setting them aside to dry; and cleaning the brushes, the glass mixing palettes and the floor. She did the chores, while I had the joy of just creating new and exciting compositions

The architect designer for the interiors of the vessel only gave me the size for the paintings and no other instructions. Both he and Ted Arison trusted me more than I trusted myself.

My sixteen murals for the M.S. *Imagination* consisted of forty-eight oil paintings. During this process, Herman would sometimes watch me work. He had not previously been exposed to or interested in art, but he learned to enjoy abstract paintings, especially mine, for their color, motion and energy.

Just one month after we met at Rancho La Puerta, we walked along our favorite beach path. We sat down by a deserted lifeguard tower, enjoying the view of Catalina Island across the sea. Both the sky and the water were the same brilliant blue. We chatted there for a while, and then he pulled me closer, looked at me seriously, and said:

"Why don't we go to Las Vegas next weekend and get married at the little church around the corner?"

I was flattered and surprised.

"I am very fond of you and maybe even falling in love, but I really don't want to get married again. You could just come and live with me. My house is large. I rattle around it and I love being with you."

He took my hands and his face was close to mine when he replied: "I want to live with you for the rest of my life. We both have children and grandchildren and I think that would set a bad example for them. Why don't you think over my proposal for a week or so before you make a decision?"

Both of us were lost in thought as we walked home. He kissed me tenderly and left.

Herman wanted me to meet Marsha, Rocky and little grandson Max. The next day, after we had dinner, he telephoned Marsha and told her that he wished to bring me to their home so we could all meet. Marsha replied that she was not ready for it. When I heard that; I'm afraid Marsha seemed to morph into Marcie before my eyes.

"I am through auditioning for daughters of the men I am involved with!"

Herman told me not to be so upset. He explained to me that Marsha did not like the woman with whom he previously had a relationship, and was worried about his new one. "Please be patient, you will see that it will all work out." "I heard the very same words before and it never did work out! It gives me pause to think over your proposal of marriage."

We went out to dinner but our conversation was forced. We both were very upset.

My murals were finished. And I was thrilled with them. A huge truck transported them to Los Angeles where they were crated for shipment to the shipyard in Helsinki. The new M.S. *Imagination* was scheduled to arrive in Miami for the inaugural cruise early that winter.

I saw Herman almost daily, but there seemed to be a reserve between us. I certainly did not want to be the cause of a rift between him and his daughter, but I couldn't help contrast my own daughter's welcoming attitude towards him with Marsha's towards me.

Then, an invitation came from Marsha and Rocky for dinner in La Jolla. Herman never told me what had led up to that. With great hesitation, I agreed to go. The visit turned out quite pleasantly. Whatever had been her objections, Marsha made me feel welcome. I especially enjoyed their little boy, Max. Seven years later he would be joined by his brother, Noah.

On January eleventh 1994, Herman and I were married in the office of Rabbi Arnold Rachlis at the University Synagogue in Irvine. All our children and grandchildren were present.

We were invited for the inaugural cruise of the *Imagination,* which served beautifully as our honeymoon trip. It was a joy and thrill to see my paintings properly installed. Hundreds of passengers admired them and I basked in the compliments from Ted and Lin Arison as well as from many Carnival executives. How wonderful it was to share this with Herman, who had a perpetual smile on his face.

After our return to Laguna Niguel, we decided to remodel my six-teen-year-old house. A number of homeowners on our street simi-larly were working on upgrading their homes. I gathered information from them about the various tradesmen, hiring all the people necessary for our remodeling job. I served as my own con-tractor. It was hard work but very gratifying.

Herman meanwhile commuted to his work at John Wayne Airport, using the new toll road that made his commute a lot shorter. He kept very busy as his company built a large new hangar and office building.

Diana

One day, Diana telephoned me and urged me to please sit down as she had something to tell me. She had been to the doctor, she started to say, and I could feel the alarm rising within me. Diana never went to doctors. She was never sick. My heart began to pound.

"Mother," she said resolutely. "I have cancer and I am going to the hospital tomorrow for a procedure." Was I really hearing right? Could this really be true? My healthy, beautiful, young daughter had cancer? I was afraid to ask if she had sought several opinions, whether she had the best of all doctors.

All I could say was: "Why don't you and Everett come over and we'll all go for a walk in Dana Point harbor?" She agreed.

All four of us walked around the beautiful harbor, on an afternoon when the weather should not have been glorious, but was. I forced myself to stay upbeat and uncritical and they obviously did the same. We walked and talked and it was good.

Melissa meanwhile had changed colleges and was now at the University of California at Santa Cruz.

On Mother's Day, Diana was in the hospital and as a gift for her, I sent for Melissa to surprise her. Diana was so thrilled she thought she was hallucinating when Melissa entered her hospital room. She said it was the best present that she ever got.

Melissa graduated from UC Santa Cruz, but none of us, not even Melissa herself attended the graduation ceremony in June, wanting to spend as much time as possible with Diana. On January twenty-sixth 1999, we lost Diana.

Finding words to describe my unbearable grief and sense of loss still is not possible for me.

San Diego

Marsha and Rocky persuaded us to move closer to their home. We put our newly remodeled home on the market and it sold within two weeks. We moved to San Diego into a lovely High-rise building. The apartment has a studio space with lots of glass and light. I called it "my studio in the sky" since it is on the twentieth floor overlooking La Jolla and a slice of the Pacific Ocean. Our two dogs had to get used to riding the elevators and walking on a leash. But there is a park nearby, and it kept us walking Scotty the black Schnauzer, and Copper the Pomeranian. Poor Scotty missed his running freely and hated the leash. Later we had the chance to have him adopted by a wonderful family with six other dogs and a big yard. Though we were sad to give him up, we felt he was much better off. Little Copper now became our "only child."

Our neighbor Neha Voigt, who became a close friend, had introduced us to many people at the University of California, San Diego, which is nearby. Her late husband was the founding librarian of what today is called the Geisel Library after Audrey and Theodore Geisel. The latter is well known to children around the world as Dr. Seuss. I was commissioned to do a posthumous portrait of Neha's husband Melvin J. Voigt. It now hangs in the lobby of the spectacular Library building on the campus of the University of California, San Diego.

Nearby, at the John and Rebecca Moore's Cancer Center, my mural, "The Four Seasons," was unveiled in April 2005. It is my special memorial to my wonderful daughter, Diana Ray Rubin Daly.

My granddaughter Melissa, a High School Math and Art teacher, was married to Patrick Dunning in a wonderful ceremony in June 2006. My late husband, Norm Pierce, whom Melissa considered her only grandfather, always said: "I want to dance at Melissa's wedding," His son Ken Pierce and his wife came to the wedding and Ken danced with Melissa in memory of Norm. Herman and I were in the wedding party. Herman's children and grandchildren and a number of our good friends were also there. Melissa wore the chain with my mother's diamond, which I had given to her mother Diana. She was a beautiful bride and both she and Patrick made a handsome couple. They are very happy.

At age eighty-five I seem to be busier than ever, painting, lecturing, writing, and hope to keep it up for a long time to come with Herman by my side. I owe so much to my many wonderful friends who helped me when I needed help, taught me so much and enriched my life.

I have experienced both trauma and fulfilled dreams. At times, such as when I ran into the American consulate in Vienna to seek a visa, or when I impetuously asked Charley to marry me, I took matters into my own hands, believing that when lives are at stake, one should not feel bound by someone else's sense of propriety.

All of my experiences and all my notions of right and wrong, of justice, and compassion and my passionate love and pride for my adopted country America, helped to build my world view. In my art I was greatly influenced by Kokoschka.

An artist's most precious quality is curiosity. It has kept me young for many years, kept me searching, experimenting and never being complacent, in my life and my work.

But most of all I feel so incredibly fortunate to have a wonderful companion who makes my life complete, my husband Herman.

Sometimes when I remonstrate with Melissa about her desire to not only teach, but to pursue an artist's life, she laughs at me.

"Grandma," she says, "You have only yourself to blame."

Melissa Daly

Hilda and Melissa

Mr. and Mrs. Patrick Dunning

Epilogue

"Der Anschluss" is a German word for "connection," which was proclaimed by Hitler

On March 13 1938, after his troops had invaded Austria. It was the beginning of Hitler's Empire.

Historians believe that the Allies made a grave mistake in not stopping Hitler at that point in time. He destroyed Europe and caused the deaths of not only six million Jews, but also sixty million other Europeans.

William Shirer, American correspondent and author, in Europe at that time, wrote that Americans had so little interest in the fate of Austria, that he had difficulty persuading CBS to allow him to report the story of the "Anschluss" on the his radio program.

Kurt von Schuschnigg, Chancellor of Austria, was imprisoned by the Nazis after the Anschluss in 1938 until May 1945. He spent time in two concentrations camps. After the war he was detained by the Americans until 1947. Later he was allowed to immigrate to America, where he was a professor at Washington University in St. Louis. He moved back to Austria and died in 1977.

About the author

Hilda Pierce, born in Vienna, fled to England in 1938 after Hitler invaded Austria. Her odyssey continues in New York, Chicago and California. A successful painter, she lives with her husband and little dog in their San Diego studio residence.

For viewing her paintings please go to her website: www.Hildapierce.com
e-mail: Hildapierce@aol.com

978-0-595-42530-
0-595-42530-5

Printed in the United States
98077LV00004B/1-111/A